Homage to

P. J's

MYSTERY

BY
PATRICK QUINN

Published by Patrick Quinn Books.
9 Sorrento Heights,
Dalkey, County Dublin
Ireland

First published in 2006

ISBN: 0-9553164-0-5

ISBN: 978-0-9553164-0-1

CONTENTS

ACKNOWLEDGEMENTS

Five people were of great help Mrs Marjorie Fitzgibbon RHA who gave guidance with the continuity that kept everything from going to pieces, Morgan LLewellan, Betty Noonan and my nephew Aidan Quinn who kept me computer wise, I would also like to thank my old friend and neighbour, Professor John Cokely of Trinity College

FOREWORD

Patrick Joseph Quinn must be one of the few truly renaissance men of our time. He was born in Dublin and although he spent forty years of his life in America, he kept a residence here in Dublin where most of his family live. I first met him at an artist's exhibition in Dublin and, being a professional Sculptor myself, our initial conversations always seemed centred on the arts. However, I was a little dubious when he asked me to look at his paintings, fearing that at best he might be a talented amateur, which would have put me in an embarrassing situation.

This however was not to be the case. I was stunned at his talent, which I really should not have been. Patrick has been a student of the great American artist Louis Busta and has had several successful one-man shows in the States under his belt. Hopefully we will be seeing a show of his here in Ireland. His interests are far ranging and though twenty years spent at sea as a Master Radio Electronics Officer may partially account for this wide-ranging literary knowledge, he has also enjoyed journalistic success. He is an expert house restorer an inveterate traveller and enjoys poems. What more can I say? His story will emerge from this, his first book, which I found absolutely fascinating. How someone with talent to burn could have got himself in such a tangled web of mystery and survived says much of the man and we are privileged for being allowed to read these experiences.

MARJORIE FITZGIBBON, RHA

CHAPTER ONE

'The smiles, the tears
of boyhood years'

Moore

My father was a stranger in the big city: He hailed from Portadown, Northern Ireland and never quite mastered the local Dublin dialect. My earliest memories were tip toeing slowly on the hot stones along the strand at Bray with him, in expectation of a plunge into the sea on a sunny summer's day walking together along the shore, me copying his large steps where there was wet sand. I would push my feet down under where it was warm.

Often he mentioned how he would have liked to have a life at sea he made it sound so magical that a part of my life was rooted in those conversations. Perhaps it was because I so seldom got to talk to him. Politicians and revolutionaries in those days had little time for family. This was intensified by the fact that I, the youngest in a family of seven children, really knew little about him and these brief moments with him became larger than life in my mind

Of Mother's lineage I have no record. She was from Ballycanew, Co. Wexford and her maiden name was McGrath. Father was in his zenith in 1922-23, three years before I was born. He was a public schoolteacher, Secretary of the Irish Republican Brotherhood, one of the founders of the Central Savings Committee and President of the Irish National Teachers Organization in 1922, and a known Dublin character in the twenties. He was an old man when I was young and died when I was fourteen.

Living on a teacher's wage in those days was not easy. Mother was amazing. She always had nourishing food on the table, so no problem there. Teachers were paid monthly, so many had to budget carefully. Though temperate, father liked a social drink. It is said that one is not a good driver until one has had an accident. I think one has to visit a Pawn shop to know the value of frugality and the honourable ethic of saving.

Because father was so generous there was a strange incident for a man of father's stature. On one occasion, he thought it important to dress up a poor boy of Jewish parents. The boy said he wanted to be a Catholic, He could not have gone for confirmation unless he got a new special confirmation suit of clothes. The boy actually turned up for confirmation in his old clothes, having pawned the new ones to my father's expense and annoyance.

He had had other unexpected expenses and was a week away from his monthly salary. He was obliged to pay a visit to the man with the 'three brass balls' (Pawnbrokers always displayed three brass balls outside their shops to show their occupation.) George Anderson, 50, Marlborough Street. Pawnbrokers had a great impact on Dubliners in those days, as had the thousands of pawn shops on others in the country. There are now less than a hundred. We stood there, father's head buried in a newspaper in the queue outside on a foul wintry morning.

Children were not allowed inside. I waited as the rain turned to hail. My coarse tweed trousers cut to the knee, showed a red band of flesh abraded by course tweed trouser edge torn by wind and hail that. (I had not yet been 'lifted' into 'longers' which in those days was a sort of Dublin Barmitzva occasion) caused a pink rash known as ire, which irritated the flesh insufferably. A week later, I saw Father absent minded reaching for his beautiful silver watch which had been presented to him. Of course it was not there. With a growing sadness at the age of five, I became aware of the reason for the visit to the shop and got my first lesson in the value of money. When the first of the month arrived, spirits were high again, I saw him holding the redeemed watch with his index finger and rubbing his thumb over the glass surface as if to assure himself that the watch would stay with him.

Father was constantly aware of the hardship that some families had to endure, especially those that he knew from his teaching. He had little respect, or should I say he had disrespect for riches or pomp or ceremony and bowed his head to the Pope only. Today we use the equity on our home to borrow money, in the 'good auld days' the equity in the pocket had to do. Life is such a big experiment from hour to hour from minute to minute, when we are young. I asked myself, notwithstanding the fact that father was one of the founders of the Irish Central Savings Organisation, why was there not a 'safety valve', or what they call 'egg money' in the country in our home? Did father offer everything and confirm nothing? Not at all: he was in fact well organised in those hard times

A change in thinking, for the man in the street to try to avoid poverty, was to come from the government no less and certainly for the better. Educate the people to save something, even if it's only a shilling a week, became an ethic worth striving for. It was in 1925 that the government inaugurated a savings committee to be operated through the schools. It was called The Central Savings Committee and was established to push the sale of a new series of Irish saving certificates. The plan was welcomed by the INTO and father, who was a member of the executive, was appointed to represent the Organisation's Committee. It was in that capacity that he served for the next ten years.

During this time he was away from home like a sailor. He went around the counties addressing many meetings of teachers and groups of employers and workers on the personal and national level extolling the advantages of a thrift movement. It was very successful. In fact, he may have visited most of the 2,500 national schools which took part in the scheme. The Minister and the Central Savings Committee congratulated the teachers on the assistance they had so willingly given in this important social work. The aim was to look to the future. Theodore Roosevelt was quoted

"Extravagance rots character, train youth away from it. The habit of saving money stiffens the will and brightens the energies".

In those times, in the twenties, being in politics was not for sissies. People were more aggressive hoping to save the country and religion, both were in jeopardy. Day to day life was different. If a man was suspected of being a homosexual he became a welcome and easy target for a 'beating up' in public toilets. Father frowned upon any of us who paid too much attention to dress. Brown boots versus black. Horses pulling the last of the trams were treated cruelly. People felt sorry for the horses and preferred to walk at times than pay a fare to see them whipped. 'Be as aggressive as one can', was the order of the day. If a boy was timid strangers in a friendly way would try to help, and to draw him out.

The following extract (which mentions father) shows something of the humour and aggressiveness informed people could have. The Irish Independent quotes of a certain day about the first convention of Cumann na nGaedheal

"It is well to remind ourselves that the police reports were occasionally jaundiced. Mallon's unrestrained contempt for a certain class of nationalist became most evident when he read in Griffith's United Irishman the long list of individuals said to have been present at the first convention of Cumann na nGaedheal. He did not believe, he said, the representation was anything like as elaborate as was said; this was mere space-filling copy. All the Dublin men named had been seen at different places and at different times by the police on the day of the convention. The majority never put foot in Abbey Street where the convention was held in premises loaned by the Celtic Literary Society to the Transvaal Committee. Two of them were habitual drunkards, two were Corporation scavengers who spoke Irish and were over sixty years old, two were schoolboys, the Emmet Guard man was a car driver and bandmaster of the Milltown Band. Egan, Griffith and Quinn were the only bad ones. Three of the parties were so drunk at 8 o'clock that they were groping their way about. One of them who, I suspect, wrote the article spent a quarter of an hour trying to find the letter box in the door of the publishing office. Among those who attended the convention and who were concerned to advance their views about reviving the Irish language and literature there was a majority of deranged faddists"t.

I had never seen father intoxicated. There was one giveaway; when rarely he was a bit merry. He dispatched one of us for fish and chips which arrived (minus a few chips) with a strong whiff of vinegar wrapped in a newspaper. The article brought father down to mortal level in my eyes.

To return to his budgeting skills, sometimes with laughter, he was asked to his discomfort how he could not budget when he was able to publish articles for the teacher's Journal on the virtues of saving? We had both suffered winter winds, hail and rain and no doubt my father had other unpleasant feelings, so much suffering to borrow a few shillings. Life was indeed hard in the thirties. It would take a financial wizard to budget on a teacher's salary. Even so, I saw 'touchers', past pupils and beggars cross the road to father (an easy 'touch') for a few 'bob'. He never failed to give spare change.

Once he was chatting with an old lady in a black shawl who always stood at Nelson's Pillar selling papers when a poorly dressed kid shook a dirty box with a picture of a black baby on it.

Father used snuff while chatting but didn't like us to notice. He washed his own large handkerchiefs which were mostly alizarin crimson or cobalt blue. "Spare a few pennies for the black babies, Sir?" As he took a pinch of snuff he replied

"Look laddie, I've got seven white babies at home that need it more!" The boy shrugged.

"If you're hungry", he said to another, "why don't you work?" "Because it would only make me hungrier," was the tart reply; hiding the hurt with humour of not being able to find work. We were a poor country then, but rich in culture.

There was no work. People had pride. A colleague in father's school in Francis street who had five children and whose husband had left for England to search for work, didn't turn up at a relative's wedding, nor (in fact) for Mass for some time. Her 'Sunday clothes' were in the pawn. Father redeemed them for her. A teacher's dress and appearance in school in those days was very important to dignify her position.

"A kind crayture every inch of him is yer da, son," chuckled the paper lady. "Is that true Da" I asked as father rummaged for two pennies, bought a paper and we walked away.

At the age of three, mother taught me how important it was to tell the truth. I struggled between belief and disbelief, when once, after a time of pondering, I realised she had lied. It was at our Sunday dinner, which was always at one thirty in the afternoon. It was for us an important and spirited event of the week. My sister's boyfriend had caused confusion in the kitchen by arriving earlier than mother expected. Being superstitious, that for some reason bothered her. Opening the back door she was greatly relieved to hear the 'craic' of brothers Malachi, Enda and Dermot, none the worse for drink after a visit to Ryan's billiard hall as they arrived to keep the guest company.

Seated around a large dining table, my father was proud of the wit and charm of his five sons, and two pretty daughters. He never let the conversation languish and there was many a hearty laugh while trying to make light of the hard times we were having.

"Go aisy on the buther." Ma would say during rationing. Whenever the Belleek teapot was used it was 'shamrock tea' (three leaves) and when one added milk the colour of the tea would almost disappear.(most days we had 'Maggy Rian' original margarine tasted like car grease). As the meal ended there was talk of Mr. Hitler's miracles in the German economy. He was building a 'people car' for every German, building roads as wide as the length of an Irish village road and huge 'balloons' that brought crowds across the Atlantic. Hitler had hinted at recovering German lost lands, which meant war was a possibility. We had a lot to be concerned about, not the least the 'troubles' in what we then referred to as the 'Six Counties'. We had Six County buses, six county industries, six county banks, now we have Northern Ireland, a minority controlled, pretending satellite of England in part of Ulster.

To get back to lying- Mother only drank port wine. She would sip it as if there was something medicinal about it. She had had a glass or two after all the work of getting the dinner ready and welcoming the guest. During the meal and table talk, I was swinging from a bar under the large dining table. Suddenly, at the age of two or three, I asked innocently.

"Where do babies come from Ma?" It was like as if a bomb hit the grouse pie. Grouse and pheasant were common game in County Wicklow in those days.

Father was incensing the room with his weekly Cuban cigar (no one else was allowed to puff at the table) and dropped it on the linen table cloth. My sister's boyfriend George (a dropout from Maynooth seminary and an easy target for ridicule on any subject except religion) grew pale as a hearty laugh from my brothers was waved down by my mother (who was a bit heady). Mother thoughtlessly tried to kill two birds with one stone. She made the biggest gaff one could imagine. It's in my head today, as clear as then when she said

"You have noticed the tabernacle in the church-the priest removes the Chalice from that box on the altar during Mass. That's where babies come from."

Half believing her and after a long pause, no sooner had the conversation grew louder again, than I came from under the table and said profoundly, in a doubtful tone.

"Can we wait next Sunday and see a baby falling out?" With that, I was the focus of a roar of laughter and chatter which I could not understand fully and shying away I crawled back under the table. The laughing eased to the clattering of dishes then there was a pause...

"Where's Paddy?" said Malachi with a hiccup that sent the whole table in a roar again.

"Where's Paddy gone, where is he?"

"I don't know! Look under the table."

Here a new round of laughter burst forth, while heads popped down a thousand eyes piercing me all at once. I was naturally confused but logic overtook my guilt at not believing. It did not take long to definitely connect weight loss with an arrival that was what I wanted to confirm in the first place. I was thrown a hell of a sanctimonious curve. I became shy having been lied to and laughed at and I wonder if that is always with us? I believe it is events like this that have made a lot of Irishmen of my generation bashful. Whether she intended to explain the facts of life later or not I do not know. I was the monkey that fell off the tree, a difficult moment for any child, which may go unnoticed by the adult around it.

It was shortly after this time of my life when the strangest thing happened to me. I saw a ghost, Many years later it appears that in actual fact I did, here's why and believe me; this is neither a fairy tale nor a sea story (and incidentally the difference between the two is, that, a fairy tale begins

'Once upon a time', a sea story begins

'Now this is no shit'.

At the age of four I had the most extraordinary experience of seeing a 'spirit' that any person could have had. Recently I had a letter confirming, as true, what I had seen from no less a person than Terry De Valera, a man of great character and goodness. I was reading his memoirs when my jaw fell, because he confirmed (as true) a recollection that was in my mind for many years. I wrote to him about my childhood experience. He was cordial enough to reply and I am sure he will not feel it amiss if I show the correspondence, as it may support experiences in our minds for years that others also may have had.

It was a cold night but the sweat rolled down my forehead in terror at seeing a spirit. It is difficult to express my own impatience when I want to do so in trying to describe what we saw that awful night. Any fruits of education or logic which I may have just wither away and I am left thoughtless with a feather in my stomach.

It was November 1929, when mother, brother Malachi, sister Sheila and two friends and I were returning from Ballycanew, County Wexford, mother's birthplace. Malachi was driving. It was a cold winter's night when the car broke down in the Glen of the Downs, Co. Wicklow.

My father would drive a car with his shoulders hunched forward, jogging resolutely along as if he was ready to pull out a whip and whip it. My brother on the other hand, then a teenager, drove in a way more to impress us, by getting to a destination as fast as possible, as if to prove his invincibility. My sister Sheila when in the car made us laugh at times. Once when we were almost in the ditch she was really 'putting it on' to suggest that Malachi my brother couldn't drive.

"Let me out, let me out, I'm not staying in this car, holy God! Let me out." When we chided him he would put on an expression of countenance peculiar to himself when anything displeased him. He scoffed,

"What is the matter, what's this whim about now?" he put on a jackass Brit. accent to tease a friend, Chris. For the most part we had a great time, until the car broke down.

"It's the clutch that's gone west; it's in gear but won't move. Can't do anything about that," Malachi said lighting a cigarette, while mother, annoyed, pushed him out of the car into the cold night to smoke.

"Leave the engine running to keep warm," Malachi said, shivering. So there we were, stuck for the night.

The trees moved in the wind and rain. We couldn't even call Da to let him know we were safe. I can still remember what the forest looked like my sense of awareness became acute. Slowly the wind ceased, everything became quiet as the low mist on the road began to burn off with a slight odour of tar and dead leaves. It was that time around four o'clock in the morning when nurses are aware of most people dying. We had been there about an hour when the empty engine stopped. Very soon we were shivering. Then it appeared, that ghost, (or whatever you want to call it) about ten metres in front of us, a woman all in white. Dumb and awe struck for moments suddenly we all spoke in consternation and terror, but none of us listened. We were too scared. Then eight metres in front of us, the woman suddenly turned to her right and disappeared. Malachi opened the window to see better and make more sense of it. Sheila froze suddenly she uttered a piercing shriek to which the forest re-echoed, unnerving us all the more. I looked with stupefaction, unable to speak.

"Ma! what is it?, Ma Ma, what is it?" then there was the mute stillness of fear.

Chris Smith got out of the car and said that she would try thumbing a lift. I tried to convince her to stay, saying,

"We haven't seen a car pass for a long time and it's cold outside." I felt we were losing one of the 'pack' in a bad situation and said

"we need you, we need you." She said she would phone father and send help. She disappeared in the night, arrived home safely and help came the next morning.

When we arrived home, father was extremely anxious to know what had happened to delay us... We paid little heed to this as we were even more nervous and the lot of us tried to explain to him (all at the same time) what we had seen. Father said he would contact the Wicklow papers and find out if there were a similar experience recorded in this 'ait aerach' (airy place in other words a haunted area) which I guess was all he thought he could do to help quieten us down. I was sent to bed. I slipped under the blankets and pulled them around my shoulders. Somehow my soul seemed frozen as well as my body after that frosty night. We received news and evidence within the week of these appearances from a Wicklow newspaper, by people who had answered Father's query. I had not given much thought to this over the years other than a reminder every time I passed the spot in the Glen. One would think that such a story would have been told over and over but in fact it was the very opposite, it was never spoken about in the family. My mother could not mention the subject without becoming unnerved. Recently, while reading Terry De Valera's memoirs, I became aware that his experience was akin to mine. He explained in correspondence quoted here.

A very good friend of mine told me an interesting story of the spot about which you have written to me. In the year 1927 there was a certain Sgt. Major Wright a drill leader returning to Dublin in his car in February 1927. The car, it seems skidded and overturned and poor Wright was impacted on the steering column and died in the ditch on or near the very bad bend on the old main road that I think we all remember- certainly I do because I hated that bend. He was wearing a white coat. He (or his ghost) was seen by my friend's close relative a year to the very day i.e. February 1928. The same Sgt. Major Wright was a very well known figure at the time. He taught drill in many schools including my eldest sister who left school in June of 1929!! Over 75 years ago now! The white coat was obviously male not female as your story seems to suggest. Your story adds up in many ways to the details my friend told me many years ago.

In those days we had an absolute belief in heaven and hell as if it were India or China. Religion was a way of life. We believed in ghosts. For good or evil we, mother, brother, sister, friend and myself each and everyone; saw the ghost of a man and not a woman! The dead walked and we accepted the presence. 'Dia linn'.

CHAPTER TWO

Within the family circle

My father was born into a large family of twelve siblings, in Portadown. This is a town where loyalists feel that a battle won is just that and seem confused as to why, after only three hundred years, people are forgetful of it. These very Orangemen, with unsocial bowler hats (looking like the Imperial dome of Rome or German WW2 helmets and 'banned in Russia') and silk status umbrellas, march every Twelfth of July, beating Japanese-like oversized drums to make their point until their fists became bloodied from the thudding. It all looks like a big play until one notices the grim faces. Fife bands, pipe bands, choruses and loads of banners with King Billy on his high horse nudging them on. It's Lilliputian in the extreme.

In my father's youthful days he would go to school with a sandwich in one pocket and the other full of stones, (which most children learned to throw with accuracy) just in case he was set upon by loyalist children, who were the majority in his neighbourhood. Today, decades later, the police, from time to time protect the children going to Catholic schools with the use of armoured cars. Nothing unfortunately has changed. The hope of Nationalists was that some day they would outnumber the Unionist at the ballot box or that the United Nations would police an election in the whole of our island.

On 16th December 1916 father put himself forward for a position in the C.E.C. of the INTO. He wrote in the Irish School Weekly.

"Work for the Organisation should be measured by the opportunities given and in the case of men in possession of originality, energy and initiative, of the opportunities created. A feeling of permanency on the C.E.C and the development of "pocket Boroughs" are hurtful to the Organisation generally, and a bar to progress. Patrick. J. Quinn, Black Pitts National School, Dublin.

Tracing his early days my sister, Eva Quinn, now in her eighties and a

French Daughter of Charity in Blackrock, found a gap of eleven years for which we could not account. It is not good mental hygiene for a family to have life secrets among themselves, I decided in my retirement to set about finding the missing activity during those hidden years this was part of the " raison d'être" for this work. The above extract from the Irish school weekly gave us a date and location to start filling in the missing parts.

Within the family circle and not aired in public, we were told all our lives that father had been in the priesthood and left. I was prompted to believe that my father may not have been. When I returned from the USA in 1995 to retire in Dalkey, I set about finding out when and where he was during these eleven years around the turn of the century,

Mother told us from time to time that the day before his ordination as a priest, he decided it was not for him and after years of study he quit. As a result, his brothers and sisters, my uncles and aunts, (eleven in all) either distanced themselves from him or vice versa. As far as I know none of my sisters or brothers met or corresponded with any of our uncles or aunts.

This was not strange in those censorious times; for example, if a man married in a Registry Office he would be dismissed from a University position or indeed from any high office. It was a 'single minded service' in the thirties and forties and on a similar subject. to quote the Papal Nuncio:

"It is because they have not lost their fidelity to the Mass that the Irish have maintained the faith of their forefathers. In Dublin alone it is said that 40,000 hear Mass each day".

Sometimes when I see the name Quinn, spelt with two N's (one 'n' used to be the money side of the clan), whether they be achievers or rogues, it passes my mind that he or she might be a relative. This is more a reflection of living alone, a problem I have difficulty solving. Returning to live in Ireland with a foreign accent, leaving friends abroad, after many years is a challenge. One is really coming to a new social involvement where it seems the aged are secluded from each other more than in most societies. It appears to me that loneliness is a real problem for the elderly here in Dublin. There are no senior centres that I know off with class, as social activities such as there are in France and California,

Family members visit parent's graves once a year and from time to time mention how we have eleven uncles and aunts whom we have never met. If I was opening a 'can of worms' so be it. In those days it was a great shame to leave the 'cloth'. In fact, because of father leaving the order (if that was the case), we only became aware of one uncle named Peador, who lived in Glasgow. We had an aunt, a reverend mother in Seville, who was killed during the civil war and is buried there. The rest apparently had no communication with father. There was a silence or evasiveness whenever they were mentioned by us as children. Religion and nationalism were somehow one and the same when I was young, as it is in Bush's fundamentalist Zionist Christian regime in America today.

Did father go from a religious vocation to that of a revolutionary? Was the personality of a priest seduced to the impersonal circle of the IRB? There were no photos or records of him as a student, yet mother always insisted he had been in a religious order and had left. Was he at sea (my fondest memory of him was his love of the sea), or even in prison, not at all unlikely for a revolutionary in the North? He may have gone on search and destroy missions which he was not proud of and might later have been ashamed of or was he, as mother says, a student for the priesthood? This was probably the most likely case, but I'm not sure. I do know he never missed Mass on Sundays and carried a rosary in his pocket. I tried to view the world he was living in by first looking at the IRB and thinking of those times for some clues.

The existence of any secret society whose object was the establishment of an Irish Republic by any method, political or otherwise, was a criminal offence in occupied Ireland. One could be a very good citizen only interested in the maintenance of good social order; one of the thousands of daily Mass goers and because of a plea of patriotism, a natural instinct and the spirit of the age, he could be fighting inclinations towards being engaged in 'criminal' activities.

It would appear that five revolutions in two hundred years should have been ample evidence that no one believed the Brits could reform or that we could get some kind of devolution. They were only interested in their bellies and what's below them. They didn't give a hoot about the remnants of the Gaelic civilisation or the Irish people as we are. We decided that there were three realistic ways to talk to the Brits; down the barrel of a gun, with the cutting edge of a pike, or the sharpened tip of a hurling stick.

The Indians, like us, gave blood to the Empire to have their lands stolen never to be returned. Pacifists say Gandhi's ideas and actions got the Brits out of India, when in fact it had more to do with the knife. They could not trust their servants when sleeping and never knew if they were going to 'wake up dead' knifed in the back beside their wives! It was as simple as that. It was the knife that lost the Jewel in the Crown. I apologize that I must digress again to get to understand father's thinking at the time to see what he could have been doing for the eleven years...

In the 17th century the priesthood was recognised as being mostly responsible for insurgency and all priests were considered rebels and were 'on the run' to avoid being sentenced to death, which was part of Cromwell's bloody reckoning. Hedge schoolmasters were better off than the name implies or from the paintings of the time which usually portray a group under a tree with another on watch. They had classrooms sometimes in schools and it would be a very warm day before they would come near a hedge. If you helped or even knew where a priest was and did not tell the authorities it was a capital crime. A wolf's head or a priest's would fetch five pounds from the authorities. This was to last until 1745 when Catholics, mostly peasants and dispossessed farmers, could be baptised openly and go to worship; although harassed by many Protestants who were the possessing. Even so there were many Protestants in the North who had their own societies for a free Ireland and many joined the 'United Irishmen' which was founded by them.

What a turn of events from those times and Rome's attitude in father's youthful years. In 1848 the Phoenix Society was founded by Jeremiah O'Donovan Rossa and James Stephens in America with the aim of attacking Britain through Canada. The clergy were successful in having the Society suppressed and sometimes resulting in its leaders being jailed. Meanwhile a stronger movement came to the fore The Irish Revolutionary Society which, in time came to be called The Irish Republican Brotherhood, the forerunner of the old IRA. This was a vast militant revolutionary secret society whose object was to get the Brits out of Ireland and to have our own Republic outside the British Empire. It was started by Luby and Stephens in Dublin in 1858. My father at the turn of the century was, I believe, in the middle its circle and may have left Portadown for Dublin to be more involved.

An oath was taken

"I, John Doe in the Presence of Almighty God, do solemnly swear allegiance to the Irish Republic now virtually established; and that I will do my utmost, at every risk, while life lasts; to defend its independence and integrity; and finally that I will yield implicit obedience in all things, not contrary to the laws of god, to the commands of my superior officers. So help me God".

Now, although the Organisation made rapid headway among people of various denominations, the weight of the Catholic Hierarchy scourged the movement and the members were excommunicated. This came about because until fairly recently we had no Cardinal, no political voice in Rome. We were represented by a foreign Cardinal from Westminster, London, who had a strong Catholic congregation and had sworn allegiance to the Queen and the British Empire.

Because there could be no secrets before the father confessor, no one could get absolution if they took the vow of secrecy. What effect would this have on a student five years into the priesthood who had to decide between

God and country?.He went to a Catholic School in Portadown possibly the same one where recently children had to have police protection. We are not looking at decades of suffering, but centuries of the same treatment for Catholics.

The family was told by mother that father left the seminary after six years (eleven years unaccounted for) into the priesthood. It could have been for the 'petticoats' (neighbours used to remark how beautiful mother was) but it seems more likely that his calling to defend our country became more important than the priesthood if he ever was in it.

Catholics had two authorities to contend with, the Brits and the confessional. Archbishop Cullen, who had seen the horrors wrought by the French revolution when living in France, was very much against the IRB and condemned it with a passion. However the Jesuits would have none of this nonsense and they made an exception. The Society of Jesus said something to the effect that:-

The ideals exposed gave moral sanction in keeping with their actions (revolution) that are those of the IRB.

This realism made sense for members who may have had pangs of conscience It rid them from the burden and fear of falling into being-double oathed men or women. The religious opinion manufactured by Westminster Cathedral for Rome of Irish freedom fighters went 'down the drain' because of the Jesuit's support. The political and philosophical genius of the Jesuits' prevailed. They, being the front rank of the church called the shots for the people and the people listened.

It may be a simplification to say that when the words 'Sinn Fein' (ourselves alone) were first used most organisations, including the IRB and young priests were happy to get on the bandwagon with that name. To quote from a letter written by Seamus Macmanus to the Irish Independent newspaper in the year 1910

In this connection the young clergy who had come out of Maynooth deserve a special word of praise. They were highly patriotic. They helped to propagate the national doctrine seen in the eyes of the older conservative clergy at great risk to themselves at a time when we were Ishmaelites of Ireland. The older clergy were entirely with the wish-washy Parliamentary party and we were considered firebrands. As an example of the courage of these young priests I would recall an incident that took place on the occasion of the annual Convention of Irish National Teachers that met at Sligo in one of the first years of the century. At the time I was no longer a teacher but was present as an invited guest with Thomas Ban. He got alarmed. Anconannon and about half a dozen priests of whom I remember the following: Father Tom Kelly who afterwards died on the Riviera, Father Hynes who became

Rector of Galway University, Father Moran who was later Parish Priest of Clare-Galway, I took up the programme as we sat down to the banquet with which the Convention wound up and noted that the first toast was to the health of the King of England. I called the attention of my fellow guests to the matter and a delegation of us went to the President to protest. A Unionist from North-East Ulster, whose name I can't remember pointed out that we could not approve of such an un-Irish act. He got alarmed and said he would alter that. He called the Vice -President James McGowan of Dromahair who refused to cancel the toast. Ten or twelve of us then trooped out, creating a sensation and leaving a long blank space at the high table. Next morning's papers not only in Dublin but in London made of it a week's sensation and a long controversy ensued. There were questions in Parliament about the insult to the King and the matter caused consternation in the empire! But never again was the Kings health proposed at an I.N.T.O. Convention. The bad habit of drinking to the King of England, which had prevailed at many an Irish function was practically, put a stop to then-.

On 16 March 1918, Father wrote the following letter which I thought was very much to the left. Was he a Red so to speak? Would that be the reason for the missing period? He ended his letter "all for each and each for all"? That he was a red was most unlikely even though Communism was in fashion. He was an active mover for the INTO to amalgamate with the Unions. On seeking election to the CEC of the INTO, he wrote the following letter to the Irish School Weekly:

Ladies and Gentlemen-As a candidate for the above position I beg to solicit your votes at the forthcoming election.

For upwards of twenty years I have been in close touch with the labour movement and well known to its leaders. During all that time I have held the conviction that organised labour was the coming power, and that the teachers, in order to secure the full benefit of popular sympathy, should officially link up with trades unionism. Year after year, defeated but never discouraged. I have brought forward motions to this effect at the local association meeting. Since the special Congress last autumn, this great advance has been made. Our organisation is now a recognised unit in the present world movement of democracy. With our members getting into step with modern progress, adequate remuneration for our work and satisfactory conditions of working, are bound to come. It will take time to permeate our organisation with the principles of discipline and self-sacrifice of fully-developed trade's unionism.. But in proportion as this education proceeds will our enemies begin to dread us.

Although seeking the position of assistant representative, my desire is to see the term "assistant" and "principal" deleted from the organisation rules and literature, the necessity for unions removed and all members recognised only on the common status of teachers. This is the true trade union principle and can only be secured by the abolition of "grades". Each qualified teacher is entitled to "living wage", increments during satisfactory service until a decent maximum is reached. As in every other trade or profession, the supervision work income should be proportionate to the amount of responsibility. Further elucidations of principles or policy are not necessary at present.

Should your votes place me in the responsible position I seek, neither time nor energy, nor any ability or experience, I have nor any ability or experience I may possess will be spared on your behalf. With you alone lies the power to selection and whether in the ranks or above them, I will continue to work in the hope that the organisation will realise and live and act up to the great trades union motto "Each for all and all for each"- I beg to remain yours faithfully

Patrick J. Quinn

Teachers were enthused by his campaign. The Editor, Irish school weekly   Oct 10 th 1910.

"Comparisons are always ticklish things to deal in, but we have no fear of ex citing jealousy anywhere when we say that of all the speeches delivered at the Mansion House meeting on Friday evening, Mr P. J. Quinn's was the most effective. It was a thoroughly realistic statement of the woes of the teacher's position by a man who knew it from experience, but its seriousness was relieved by many humorous flashes and thrusts which never missed their mark. We congratulate Mr .Quinn on his very fine efforts.

The hopes and aspirations expressed in the making of the Teachers Club in Parnell Square saw father standing up in the crowd, driven by the guide lines that helped make the dream of an INTO deluxe club a reality. In a letter written to the Teachers Journal, father included the following sentence:

"When we see over £20.000.00 lying almost idle it is difficult to have patience with hagglers who mistake parsimonious huckstering for financial genius".

Dad was never lost for words when he became impatient. The full text of the letter is worth quoting here as it shows his sense of commitment to whatever cause he championed. The following article rebutting lines taken out of context gave father the opportunity to restate with emphasis his position. My sister Eva sat in the warm parlour with rainy sleet and grey skies outside. She typed the article over many times before it was ready. I include it here because of its interest in the times and struggles of the teachers in getting organised to have a decent wage. If the reader finds it a distraction, please skip it. * The Teachers Club grew successfully over the years and today it is a showpiece in Parnell Square

Sir-At the recent Congress there was a reference to the proposed establishment of a Teachers' Club in Dublin. During Congress, clear thinking would seem vain endeavour and almost out of place. Amidst the torrents of voluble rhetoric rushing through a highly charged atmosphere any attempt at clear exposition or reasoned statement would almost make confusion worse confounded. Long-winded orations conveying nothing and meaningless stump speeches on subjects already talked threadbare and confined to the same stock group who monopolise most of the discussions, are the usual characteristics of the Easter Week proceedings. The columns of your Journal, therefore, form a better platform and atmosphere for calm discussion. The following views on the above subject, may be challenged, contradicted or controverted, but they are my own. No one else is responsible for them.

The Dublin teachers have long felt that a club for the exclusive use of teachers is a necessity. Several attempts within the past twelve years have been made to establish one, but lack of cash or the difficulty of securing suitable premises always nipped the project in the bud. A couple of years ago a suitable house-36 Parnell Square-came into the market, and the C.E.C. were induced to invest £2000 in its purchase. This action gave hope that the dream of all progressive teachers was about to be realised. Another thousand pounds was spent in repairs, doing up, etc so that at the present moment, there is a premises suited in every detail to the intended purpose It should be stated at once (1) that these premises are an asset of the organisation which will readily realise, at any time, the total amount expended plus a profit; (2) that over £20,000 of the funds of the organisation are not invested at all and are drawing a mere deposit account interest.

I might point out that the ideas underlying this club are as follows:-

(1) The Club is to have no connection with any particular Branch of the Organisation.

(2) The membership of the club is to comprise every teacher in the Organisation who voluntarily becomes a member according to its rules.

(3) The club is to be registered under the Club's Registration Act and to be governed by a committee elected by and responsible to the members, with officers, trustees, etc., as required by the Act

(4) As city members would use the premises more frequently, a larger subscription be charged to them than to members residing in the country, but equality of club rights for all.

(5)-Non-members of the club to have no right of entrance or use of the premises. The club may hire to any branch or any body, rooms for branch meetings at the usual rates. No Branch can claim right of free use of premises for meetings or other business.

(6) In addition to the usual billiard and other amusement rooms, there will be an educational Library, Reading room and reference rooms; one flat set apart for exclusive use of lady members, and one common room in which the use of any language except Irish will be forbidden. There is a large garage at the rear of the premises as well as sufficient space to erect a Congress Hall.

Such is the skeleton of the proposed club as I understand it. It will be autonomous and all members will have equality in the selection of the governing committee. It will be a registered corporate body and as such will, through its trustees, be the direct tenant of the C.E.C The teachers through the C.E.C. are investing their own money in a premises which will be let directly to themselves, or to as many of them as chose to become members for their common benefit. To any progressive mind the possibilities of such a club are beyond measure. At present many Dublin teachers are in lodgings where the surroundings are against successful private study or preparation for work. The club library will supply the want. When many country teachers visit Dublin they have nowhere to spend a wet or dull evening, or search for or meet friends except the taverns. These resorts are expensive and not intellectually elevating. The motor car has brought teachers living fifty or sixty miles from Dublin into touch with the city. Shopping and sales are an attraction. And a resting place where friends can meet and quiet conversation is secure becomes a necessity. Appointments can be made and social intercourse between town and country teachers cannot fail to improve and elevate all concerned. The club will supply all these wants. There is no doubt but that in time this club will become one of the best equipped and most comfortably furnished in Dublin.* The Rent therefore should be a reasonable interest on the total outlay recollecting that the prospective tenant is indirectly the landlord. When we see over £20,000 lying almost idle it is difficult to have patience with hagglers who mistake parsimonious huckstering for financial genius

Is mise
Patrick J. QUINN
10 Ring St., Inchicore.

CHAPTER THREE

Schooldays

"*T*he archbishop of Dublin Dr Bernard assured us that in his boyhood only three things had been regarded as necessary in a boy's school—a boy, a book and a cane"*

On the way to school for my first day, mother could not convince me that I was not en route to a daily clobbering by the nuns at Goldenbridge, Inchicore. Sheila, a feisty five years older sister had just cut her finger peeling potatoes and had a big dirty looking cobweb on it to stop the bleeding; (It had a similar effect to fibrinogen in coagulating blood and was commonly used), assured me so with glee before we left the house.

Sisters were the worst to deal with as I was bullied by one and spoilt by the other. My brothers let me be. A few years back my sister Eva the nun was giving advice to my niece on how to bring up her child. Ethne got annoyed and said

"How do you know you never had any kids"? Eve instantly said

"Well I was the one that brought up Paddy!" I said to myself listening to this- at least someone tried to bring me up.

"The Sisters of Charity have *no charity* and the Sisters of Mercy have *no mercy,* Paddy" Sheila scoffed,, a mocker, she made no bones about telling me that I was ugly and often reminded me that 'children should be seen and not heard' as if she were that much older. Mother was not to be trusted even though I loved her. I categorically refused to go. I tried bravely to show my independence so resolutely that, on the road, I accidentally banged my head against a metal lamp pole and arrived in school half-stunned with a huge blue lump on my forehead. Every eye in the class was upon me. I was ushered (I suspect now, it was because of my father's relationship with schools) to an appropriated desk with a toy by a well-intentioned young nun; it backfired, as the new kid on the block, the last thing I needed was to appear grandiose. I got stage fright and felt like crawling under the desk. The first few days I wished at times I had Prince, my dog, to play with. As the week passed however I sat at a back desk making friends with the boys to the rear of the class.

My memory of Goldenbridge is that of an over-crowded school and an under staffed group of nuns handling the roughest Inchicore types such as the gangs from the Keogh Barrack slums. It was common to have between forty and fifty pupils in the class. Today we have problems of violence towards teachers with only twenty pupils in a class at times and some find it necessary to seek counselling for tension. In the thirties there was no six months break for a 'nervous breakdown' as there is today. It was all go for the nuns, and they were heroic in their duty.

Sibling rivalry was strong but ceased when father was present, not because he was strict but because he was venerated and our own personalities faded in his presence. He was Pope and Prime Minster. An incident occurred when I was three or four that impressed me. I was lying on the floor with a paper palette drawing a ship from memory when I gave it to my brother Enda (an amateur boxer) to improve it.

Enda worked magic with the pencil and I was raving about having the picture and marvelling at his work. I was about to grab the pallette from him when he heard father's footsteps in the hall. I looked forward to showing it to father when suddenly Enda tore the page from the palette, ruffled it and put it in the fire. Enda was the smartest one in the family but he had a sense of humour which made us seem foolish at times and he was fond of a practical joke. I became confused and hurt and could not understand why he was ashamed that father might see it or if he was having a joke on me. After I slowly recovered I picked up the palette and tried to draw what he had done from memory. Father who was reading the paper, became amused and said with a smile (praise was rare)

"Paddy that looks good, now get your crayons and put the Irish flag on it" My father had one fault as I see it now, which was, that not once did I see him open my schoolbag or question me as to how I was doing at school. I don't ever remember being asked what 'did you learn' today. Whenever I remember father I think of that incident and his expression of joy and know he was loveable. I have painted for many years and my drawing has improved by doing so, but I have never been able to take an interest in drawing since that event without remembering it as time passed. I must have been one of the most frequent visitors to our galleries when young. This I consider was a most valuable part of my education along with reading literature.

When we moved to the North side of Dublin to Belton Park, Donnycarney (next to the king of the pipers, Leo Rowsome) I attended the Christian Brothers school in Marino. They were 'a cold shower' and the queerest

bunch of half collared nobs one could meet with whom to this day I cannot come to terms. Their belief that violence was the way to correct unacceptable behaviour and control large classes was demoralizing for the weak and slow to learn, pupils who were yet intelligent and could go far if handled properly.
.

Some of us were more inspired with terror than respect for the Brothers. Like Goldenbridge School, the classes were overcrowded but at Marino the cane was habitually overused. We were rewarded with 'ear slaps' should we close our fists. One frosty morning we had been an hour in the class; the room was not yet warm when we had a shocking experience. A young slim Brother with 'bat wing' ears and a high pitched voice sweated as he caned us. Suddenly the glass-panelled door in the rear of the room was pushed open with a bang and in walked a short muscular determined young man. He paused a moment, then went to the front of the room, grabbed the Brother by the lapels ruffling him and said,

"Slap my kid brother and you'll get it, do you hear me? Cane him again and you'll get it; I'll break your bloody snozzle, do you understand, I'm warning you". He harassed the young Brother till his head with tossed hair seemed to swell looking like a red turnip, then pushed him away and left the classroom. The Brother roared threats at him as he slammed the door. We were shocked. The Brother mumbled something about gurriers and tried to quiet himself. For awhile he was so raging mad, we were afraid he would go 'bonkers' and visualized him being certified. We worried if he would tone down the caning or get worse to show his power. The tension was electric.

With our simple minds, we began to realise that life was not supposed to be like this, we had rights against punishment. Tensions evaporated as we stared at the contorted face of the brother trying to calm himself.

I, for one, was not sympathetic to the Brother (I had bruised blue fingers) but I felt a pity for the man who hustled him, because I sensed that he must have suffered when he was young to do such a terrible thing, Heaven was pitiless in those days especially for 'the backbenchers'. Walking up the hill on the Malahide road coming from Marino school I would think of books in the hope of forgetting the class and dream of becoming a writer like George Bernard Shaw. I would look forward to a good 'read' all the more dividing me from solving the real issue of the hour , the lack of application to 'rote learning' for my own benefit and to my studies. But what did all this book reading come to? For one thing it was the breath of life while growing up and made us humble and sharing and it helped us to overcome the humiliations of school. Books, newspapers and the radio were the main ways people relaxed.

Though I tried hard at times, I could not remember the answers to a lot of questions in the Catechism and often had blue fingers from caning. I was a rebellious pupil I guess. I had difficulty then and even today in understanding the meaning of 'Hail holy Queen, Mother of mercy, Hail our life our sweetness and our hope'. Attending Mass weekly these times, I am still unsure without the written word of the Creed to read. My love of the church and the truths it teaches in contrast to a 'looney' Brother makes me apprehensive writing this. I was also a bad student at mathematics, but in a more peaceful setting I became an electronic engineer.

The golden rule, which Teacher Campbell chanted as we lined up for caning after missing catechism or other questions, was:

'The little bird that can sing, and that won't sing, will be made to sing.'
This he repeated like a mantra while he enjoyed a workout caning the queue of boys. Joyce put the same tune to poetic words

'Sorry chaps it must be done, down with the pants and out with the bum.
- James Joyce

Knowing the power of the cane and often feeling it, was most depressing and made one lethargic. I did a lot of things aimlessly and arrived home jaded so the thought of pulling out my exercises later in the evening and getting ready for the next day went by the wayside in trying to forget the present day. I would take the punishment and go on spiting and hating the teacher. In all the years of schooling I cannot remember father, the schoolteacher, asking or insisting to help me with my homework. No one asked the question.

"Have you done your exercise?" Opening the door on this part of the past troubles me because I must have suppressed a great deal of emotions and nothing comes back to me voluntarily.

One great advantage I had was the treasure house of books at home. One set of five volumes in particular called 'The World's Library of Best Books" gave me more pleasure as a youth than anything else. It had extracts from the best books and was full of pictures. By reading over and over these masterpieces I gained a valuable knowledge of the great writers. Father was a Censor for Veritas (which was and still is a bookstore that supplies colleges with books) Reading increased my consciousness and gave interest and meaning to the world, I was able to go hand in hand in my imagination with great and friendly people. There was seldom a time when one of us was not reading. Sometimes we almost fought over getting the first read. 'San Michele by Axel Munthe', 'Gone with the wind', 'How green was my valley' and François Moriac were some to the favourites.

The more privileged boys sat to the front of the class and were rarely caned. From the centre to the rear it rose to a crescendo.

"There shall be weeping and gnashing of teeth" Campbell would say as the perspiration rose on his forehead, while he turned pale, breathing heavily and losing wind. The pupils to the front made grimaces and faces as if they were taking light punishment. Our caning accentuated their position and was a reminder of what could happen to them if they slid back in their studies. We at the back felt it would be easier to get out of Mountjoy jail than to move from the rear to the front.

Some had tears running down their faces if the cane hit between the joints of the fingers which was painful after five or six slashes. The fingers would turn blue and swell the next day, which was a worrisome reminder that there would be more to come.

In all those years I never played truant. One day a boy brought a note from his father saying his mother was having a baby and he could not attend. Two weeks later he was absent for a a few days, and brought a similar note saying that his mother was having another baby. The teacher questioned him. He stuck to his guns until the sniggering in the class grew so loud that he became confused and finally broke down crying like a baby himself.

"Sit down, shut up and stop making a fool of your self" Campbell cautioned but what he did afterwards to the boy, if anything, I don't know.

While taking catechism lessons we would form a queue to be questioned in the catechism or on an extract from the bible. If we answered correctly we could sit down to study, if not we were caned and went to the tail of the queue. This went on until one or two were left and I believe a lot of students developed arthritis in the fingers earlier in life because of this overacting systems. In Holland I recently read the discipline was even more severe at that time where children were often injured.

"He who only rules by terror, Doth a grievous wrong
Deep as hell I admit his error, listen to my song"

Pope?

Words to that effect cause one to wonder where the soul comes into the discipline. 'Spare the rod and spoil the child' is an Old Testament fallacy for the most part in my experience and should be read backwards.

Many successful men who went to Marino Schools have nothing but gratitude for the Brothers' disciplinary ways. They did a lot more good than harm. In my case, it took me years to learn what I should and could have done at school. I feel this also gave me an inflated opinion of those who carry degrees, because for the most part I am self-educated.

It stands to reason that if a group of men with the 'half collar' live a celibate life, besides coping with sexual problems, there is no outlet for pent-up emotion other than the 'kicks' they may get from disciplining us kids. We were faintly aware of the fact that there must have been some sad misfits among them. The majority of brothers were well-intentioned and good willed in preparing us to live successfully in a difficult and poor country, but it was possible to suffer from uncouth and heartless sadists and just remember the worst of days.

Preparation for confirmation could be a terrifying experience. We were warned that if one missed the catechism question, (one excuse for caning) the bishop would ask us to leave the church in disgrace. What should have been an oncoming joyous occasion had become one of dread and misgivings. I cried one night and was so confused next day I could not remember a word of the catechism. As I reluctantly came down the stairs on that dreary winter's morning my sister Eva (the eldest) looked at me apprehensively.

"What's the matter Paddy, you look very tired. Didn't you sleep? You know tomorrow is Saturday and we are going into town to buy your Confirmation suit and shoes and I knitted you woollen socks! Aren't you happy about that?"

"I don't want them and nothing more!" I frowned, depressed, walked into the kitchen and began to eat my porridge in silence, feeling awful. I recollected the nightmare I had; among all the hundreds of boys I could see myself walking out alone having failed. Imagine that happening after all the money my parents had spent dressing me up! How disappointed they would be, having looked forward so eagerly to giving me a memorable day. I was being punished for being slothful, spoiled with toys from family and friends.

We were told by the brothers that if we didn't understand the mysteries or other problems, *just leave it to faith.* Two things were for sure. The atom was the smallest body and was undividable and that the difference between man and all other beings was that man could make tools and no other beings could do so. Both proved false.

One climbed steps to enter Marino church which was large and costly to heat. As our class huddled together in the front pew, the bishop instead of being 'fire and brimstone' as Campbell said had kindness in his voice that surprised and put us at ease. He asked me,

"What are the sins against hope?" to which I instantly replied (having had a problem with hope).

"The sins against hope are despair and presumption." Greatly relieved, I could then have answered every question for the bishop and strangely a lot less if Campbell was waving the cane.

The unfortunate boy next to me (whom we called Smiley) got a question, a very simple one. He became speechless even though I'm sure he knew the answer. The bishop, smiled, helped him with the answer and moved on.

Smiley seldom smiled and always looked as if he was pondering a deep problem, while his mouth arched downward and he had a furrowed brow like an old man pondering death. One day Campbell got annoyed at Smiley's gloomy look and requested that each pupil must bring a funny story the following day in order for us to make Smiley laugh. Campbell told us about a British officer, Major Gough just arrived in Ireland after riding his horse all day, stopped at an Inn. He sent his aide to get some hay to wipe the sweat off the horses. The aide spoke Cockney to the Innkeeper.

"I need some aih to wipe ma master's ass." The Innkeeper replied,

"Begorrah man in this country we use paper or dry moss not Hay."

Some of us laughed but not Smiley. In fact his face was sad now and everyone felt uncomfortable. One more joke and the class was dismissed. Smiley 'bottled up' every problem and never discussed anything. Smiley didn't need jokes he would have been helped with a friendly chat.

Each had to solve his own difficulties or he was a sissie. If one hurt oneself, don't tell, because you will be either made fun of, or called stupid. I learnt that lesson the first day at school with my bumped head and when I got home my sister said.

"Will ye look at the size of the bump on his forehead, the eejit walked into a lamppost", she told everybody. This lesson stood me well...

Had the Brothers not used the cane so freely and displayed more humour, our natural love of study might have been better served but the classes were very full and hard to handle. So guidance, shepherding and free thought suffered from the severe disciplining.

Father died on the 2 April 1941.

I felt the absence of father, who never seemed to have been fully with me, which is understandable when one considers his career. I was fourteen then and remember feeling a little ashamed at myself for not caring more about his death, Looking out the window of the carriage I was surprised to notice that it was not possible to see the end of the mourners on the long street, there were so many. I realised then that father was special.

He moved to Dublin after the British controlled State-let was created in his part of Ulster and it was there I was born at 10 Ring Street, Inchicore. In 1930 we moved to 35 Bulfin Road, Inchicore. This was a larger house with a garden. It had a tub for Saturday night scrubbings.

Clothes were washed in a big sink of hot water using bars of Sunlight or carbolic soap. (powder had not been invented). After the hard chore of rubbing the soap all over the cloth, the 'ribbed washing board' was then held vertical and the clothes rubbed up and down against it, until the clothes were clean. This was a back breaking job of the week. Neighbours would peruse the clothes outside to dry. Blankets were washed in the tub, soaped over and swished around with a big stick or trampled upon which gave nice clean feet. Twisting the heavy blankets to drain the water was done by the boys. We had a 'washer woman' one day a week.

Mother and the girls were always busy and there were stacks of J.D.Williams books of patterns for dressmaking. Once I had to stand military erect while wearing a dress which was then hemmed with speed and accuracy, so Eve could rush down with chrysanthemums to the Grotto in Inchicore, for the Queen of the May altar. The clothes made were as nice as one would buy in the best shops.

Father never showed any animosity towards anyone in the North and would take the family on 'mystery' tours (when tipped of by the train driver friend of his as to where the train was going) to Portadown. Christmas was ample compensation for a lot, with the joy and wonder of it all. It was difficult to find a place in church or wall to lean on for the Christmas Mass. In the rear there was usually an odour of sweat so we pushed up front to lighted candles; flowers strewn across the altar and altar boys waving strong incense sending welcome grey clouds to the ceiling. The choir sang the Gloria in Excelsis Deo while we stood up in a military fashion. By the time the crowd had Communion (only the priests could give it then) it was almost two hours before we came from the suffocating heat to the harsh wind and cold outside. Woollen socks, jerseys and short trousers were poor windbreakers, though very warm indoors. People hung around the door outside nursing the heat to wish each other well. Bicycles were on the walls surrounding the church.

We were happy to arrive home to a warm house and a big Irish breakfast. We had dinner at three o'clock instead of the usual one' clock that day; and sat to the odour of turkey, ham and a somewhat greasy goose for good measure - a real Christmas dinner! For desert Christmas pudding laced with porter, trifle with sherry (which I found a bit heady), and blancmanges made from Carrageen Moss, which was delicious.

My brothers joked with each other and did the washing up of dishes without a murmur or a hint of a complaint, pampered all year when my sisters did the house chores. White wine arrived from father's friend and colleague in Germany, Christmas cards with French, British and other allied colours, and there were presents at the foot of the Christmas tree!

Visitors stopped by in the afternoon and evening. Across the road Jack Doyle the Boxer and his wife Movita threw hands full of coins to the crowd outside as the cheers grew louder each time. People cared! As evening came, between neighbours and friends there was only standing room in the house. The short grey winter's day passed swiftly.

I believed in Santa until I saw a drunken brawl by Santas, outside

Arnott's in Henry Street. Mother looked the other way. J. O'Leary from Inchicore gave me a burgundy bicycle supplied by a store called 'McHugh Himself' in Talbot Street. I carried it up the stairs to our crowded bedroom every night. I would wake up each morning seeing my 'flag' (it's mine) on it greet me. It was a kind of psychological 'security blanket', a 'comforter' that helped me to be my 'own man' as well as having great fun joy riding. My mind reverts to that colour as my preference when choosing a car today. Father died on the 2 April 1941.

I felt the absence of father, who never seemed to have been fully with me, which is understandable when one considers his career. I was fourteen then and remember feeling a little ashamed at myself for not caring more about his death, Looking out the window of the carriage I was surprised to notice that it was not possible to see the end of the mourners on the long street, there were so many. I realised then that father was special.

I was fourteen when father died and I regretted that all I had left of father was an obituary (Appendix I). A brother remarked, seeing my unease, as the funeral made its way to Glasnevan, "You know Paddy, you never *knew* your father". I silently agreed (as I would today), thinking he seldom was around; the remark was hurtful at the time. The funeral was the biggest Donnycarney had seen and upsetting to the Haugheys who turned away in distain as it approached their house. Father or mother never slapped any of us. In a way I probably 'lost out' not getting a flogging when I warranted it, if avoiding home study.

Among my collection of old books the one I treasure the most is a copy of Dr. Goldsmiths HISTORY of GREECE written in 1798. Going back two thousand and eighty nine years before Christ we get a glimpse into the system of education they had in the most civilized country in the world. It might invite a blush to compare the discipline and obedience of those times with the present.

Dr. Goldsmith.

To accustom the youth to early habits of discipline and obedience, Lycurgus took their education out of the hands of their parents, and committed it to masters appointed by the state. So desirous indeed, was he of having a hardy and robust race of citizens, that he began the work of education, even from the time of the mother's conception, making it her duty to use such diet and exercise, as might fit her to produce a healthy and vigorous offspring. Nay, such children as were born with any capital defect, were not suffered to be brought up but were exposed to perish in a cavern near mount Taygetus; and such as, upon a public view, were deemed to be sound and healthy, were adapted as children of the state, and delivered to their parents to be nursed with rigour and severity. From their tenderest years they were accustomed to make no choice in their eating, not to be afraid in the dark, or when left alone; not to be peevish or fretful; to walk barefoot; to lie hard at nights; to wear the same clothes summer and winter, and to fear nothing from their equals. At the age of seven they were taken from their parents and delivered over to the classes for a public education. There discipline there was still more rigid and severe. They were still obliged to go barefoot, there heads were shaved, and they fought with one another naked.

To enable them to better to endure bodily pain without complaining, they were annually whipped at the altar of Diana; and the boy that bore the punishment with the greatest fortitude came of victorious. Plutarch tells us that he has seen several children expire at this under this cruel treatment; and he makes mention of one who having stolen a fox, and hid it under his coat, chose rather to let the animal tear out his bowels than discover the theft. In order to order to prepare them for the stratagems of war, they were permitted to steal from one another; but if they were caught in the fact, they were punished for their want of dexterity. At twelve years of age they were removed in to a class of a more advanced kind. There their labour and discipline were increased with their years. They had now their skirmishes between small parties, and their mock fights between larger bodies; and in these they sometimes fought with such obstinacy, that they were seen to lose their eyes, and even their lives, before they gave u the contest. Such was the constant discipline of their minority, which lasted till the age of thirty, before which they were not permitted to marry, to go into the troops or to bear any office in the state.

The discipline of the virgins was as severe as of the young men. They were inured to a life of labour and industry till they were twenty years of age, before which time they were not allowed to be marriageable. They had also their peculiar exercises. They ran, wrestled, and pitched the bar; and performed all these feats, naked before the whole body of citizens. Yet this was thought no way indecent, it was supposed, that the frequent view of the person would tend rather to check rather than excite every irregular desire. An education so manlike, did not fail to bestow upon the Spartan women equal vigour of body and mind. They were bold, hardy, and patriotic filled with a sense of honour and military glory. Some foreign women, in conversation with the wife of Leonidas, saying, that the Spartan women alone knew how to govern the men, the boldly replied "The "Spartan women alone bring forth men". A mother was known to give her son, who was going to battle, his shield, with this gallant advice, " Return with it, or return upon it," thereby in effect telling him that rather than throw it away in flight, he should be borne home upon it dead. Another hearing that her son was killed fighting for his country, answered without any emotion, "it was for that I brought him into the world" After the battle of Leuctra, the parents of those who fell in the action, went to the temples to thank the gods that their sons had done their duty, while those whose children survived the dreadful day were overwhelmed with grief.

*Quote Irish School weekly

CHAPTER FOUR

'Out of Donnycarney'

Says I to meself, says I.

I n English Donnycarney makes no sense but the Gaelic, Domhnach ui Cearnach, if memory serves me means Cearnach's or Carney's church.

It was a long old ride on a bike from the city on a wet day, as thousands of bike riders, who took the 'width' of the road, were acutely aware in those days. If the weather was soft, it was a nice exercise to walk from Donnycarney to the city, and we saved the bus fare. We moved into n a newly built terraced house 39 Belton Park a few years before the war.

It was a two-story solid brick building with three bedrooms a nice kitchen and living room. Mother and father slept in one bedroom, four boys in the other and two girls in the smallest. The house was well furnished with carpets on the floor downstairs. Often father would surprise us by bringing home a painting or a picture for the wall until we ran out of wall space. My brother Kevin exchanged coupons from cigarette packages for a copy of the 'Laughing Cavalier' and had it framed and hung in the bedroom. It was my favourite. I marvelled at the enigmatic smile that followed one around the room and also the fine lace work. The living room was large and had a big table in it.

The view was similar to that of any terraced house. We had neat gardens with flowers, not scenic yet mostly tidy and nice. The house was solid brick so the fact that it was not detached was of no consequence, no noise or interference. The rear window looked to a long, mostly unproductive large garden where we grew rhubarb, vegetable marrow (when stuffed properly was delicious) Brussels sprouts, parsley, lots of cress for salad and mustard growing almost wild. At times half the garden was raked over to cover weeds. The spade was used sparingly, often shamefully rusting outside.

One could almost tell the day of the week by the food. Fish on Friday with colcannon, boiled bacon and cabbage on Saturday (the 'left over bacon' would be used for sandwiches on Sunday night). Sunday roast beef with roast vegetables, sherry trifle for dessert followed by tea and biscuits or cake. Monday we had leftovers. Tuesday corned beef with cabbage or Brussels sprouts. Wednesday bacon and cabbage or rabbit, Thursday whatever was available.

In ten minutes we could be in fields with a little stream to mess and play in. We built a dyke to make the stream deeper, so we could float on a plank, which quickly turned us knee deep into the water. Why not make a real boat? We folded a corrugated iron sheet beating the bow to a point and sealing the stern with plywood and tar, only to see it sink like a sieve. More mobile on dry land a butter box on each end of a plank, four pram wheels, a crude brake and a variety of left over paints. "Who's going to push?" Hey! Not me, my turn. It was like pushing a tank and when we got it to the hill it was so hard to stop that once we were pulled from the road by a Garda who gave us a caution. The fields had trees which we climbed, to have a good 'lookout' while smoking our first cigarette. They are now built upon. We seldom discussed sex as boys except in a crude way. Once when I was on the Blackrock beach with Enda a girl momentarily showed her breasts while changing to a bathing suit.

"How would I go to that girl to do something, how does one get close; you saw the way she smiled?"

"Just walk down take your cock out and put it in her hand" he jested. That was the only conversation I had about sex and the facts of life which I can remember having with anyone in the family as a boy. * MacLiammor described an experience after Noel Coward taught him the facts of life 'but he had them all wrong' he said. Both were homosexual. This is reason enough why sex should be taught in the schools.

Soon after we moved, our next door neighbour Mr Coonan, (who had lived in England and married an English girl) a bricklayer, got to work building a six feet high wall around his house, blotting out the morning sun from our garden. Mr Coonan was a dignified, cautious Longford man, five feet nine with dark hair, blue eyes, very muscular with a handsome moustache. He was a pipe smoker who took no chances as he always wore large braces *and a belt* under his mason's apron. We always referred to him as *Mr* Coonan.

Shortly after he finished the wall, he built an air raid shelter for six (though there were only four in his family). He kept stocks of canned food supplies and emergency equipment. He related his experiences of the first war with a half Longford, half-cockney accent and disagreed when we said the gas mask (every citizen was issued with one) would be enough protection. He was chatty and we gave serious thought to what he said but no one seemed to buy the idea of going underground in case the Jerries paid us a visit or more likely a return of the Brits.

We had two other neighbours worthy of note Joe Bonny who lived on Collins Avenue and Charlie Haughey (later to become Taoseach) who lived a few houses away.

Joe Bonny learned the drums in the Irish army and became a popular Dublin entertainer who played in the Theatre Royal. His daughter Monica also had her own act there on the xylophone. I went to school with his son Joe, who aspired to be a drummer like his father.

One evening he invited me to come with him to the Saint Laurence O'Toole pipe band hall at Seville Place, where his father was giving drumming drills for a competition the band was entering. My interest grew hearing the roar of the pipes a block away before entering the hall when the walls seemed to tremble. Joe, surrounded by drummers, was convincing them that instead of using a drum or the wooden table they should practice on hard pieces of flat rubber. The drumsticks would find it hard to bounce this showing up faulty beats and strengthening the fingers.

To my surprise I was given a practice chanter by the pipe major Tom Duffy. He was a piobaireacht piper, the best I have ever heard and a really kind man. It was a great loss years later when he fell on a construction site and died. I became a fair 'band' piper and soon had a uniform and set of pipes and went to different events as had done Sean O'Casey, the playwright in the same band some years before. It is believed by some that the Irish brought the bagpipes to Scotland with the Keltic invasion of the East, (the English say we brought it as a joke and our Scottish cousins haven't got wise to it yet). However, the difference between a band piper (which the general public think of when pipes are mentioned) and a good solo piper is great. As Pipe Major Macoll mentioned "Unlike most folk instruments the pipes have developed a highly complex, *written* music, which was taught in a formal manner and encouraged a competitive virtuosity not often associated with other instruments.

There are two classes of pipe music, the piobaireacht and the ceol aotrom. To the connoisseur, it is the piobaireacht or rigidly prescribed classical music which makes the piper. A man is counted a good piper if he knows four piobrochs. The gold medal given to the best player is as honoured as the Olympic gold. The ceol aotrom are the short pieces, the jigs, reels and marches. A good piper will have hundreds of these in his repertoire. "The pipes are harder to understand than women and they're impossible" Macoll said.

One evening, while practising, in walked a short pale handsome man who smoked heavily, it was Cathal Golding with his brother Noel. After a big welcome and some 'craic', Tom Duffy offered his pipes to Cathal to 'have a go'. Cathal took his overcoat off, removed a revolver from his pocket and along with some other hardware placed them conspicuously on the table and played 'Garry Owen' and finished with the 'Highland Wedding', a difficult tune. As my eye lingered on the weapon I wondered at the time if Cathal was being rash or if the whole band was in the army or both. Around 1914 pipe bands were a cover for I.R.A. Clan Ulaidh and Saint Malachi's pipe bands in were all members.

Cathal was a man of action, a great patriot who became leader of the Provisional I.R.A. I noticed his short stubby fingers found it difficult to spread over the holes of the chanter (long fingers are best for piping) and they were spotted with paint. His brother meanwhile spread lovely pieces of needle work with Irish themes on the table. These had been done by I.R.A. prisoners. I took an instant liking to Cathal Golding. Since it was a long time ago, I cannot remember how I came to get his ivory mounted pipes or if they were a gift. I have them in full trim to this day. At that time he lived on Cadogan Road, Fairview when he wasn't in jail or on the run.

Another neighbour C.A. Haughey does not bring pleasant memories to mind. I had left him out of these memoirs altogether but he did become Taoiseach and remained so for many years. I will open 'a can of worms' and give my two cents worth on what it was like growing up with the Haugheys

"*If one has power, it would be only a fool who would not use it to make money*". I was told by a friend of Charlie, that the above was a favourite remark of his to his dining guests. Some Donnycarney folks saw the Haugheys as being intoxicated by the search for power and money. The family practiced the diplomacy of bullying and certitude like no other. I was a target on one occasion and narrowly escaped a beating by two Haughey girls no less, (and yet I had never spoken to any of them) except that a kind one (perhaps the eldest), protested by grabbing the two and telling them to back off.

Why did they want to beat me up? I was not just a convenient twelve year old arse, a dog to kick to give kicking pleasure; there was hate in their eyes and I was physically afraid of their pale faced aggressive behaviour. I thought myself a good neighbour. I became afraid of them and their family. I could not understand why they would want to insult and to beat me up outside my home. I had not spoken to any of them ever (or wished to for that matter which may have been part of the problem) but had to pass their house regularly to cross over to mine. One was either 'in or out' and if you were in it was my 'buddy right or *wrong*' if you were 'out' you were an enemy. I was introduced to Charlie as a teenager by a buddy of mine, Jerry Cowan, during which he closed his fingers so I could not shake his hand properly. Was this an affront? I assumed Haughey was embarrassed because his mother had some association with a machine that made stockings, which may have been given to them by the Cowans to help them make and sell socks. Cowan asked Haughey if he had passed his B.A. Haughey replied 'no, I passed it with honours'. Yet he was of course a brilliant man but emotionally he did not seem to sit comfortably.

The mother rode a bike even in heavy weather for many years and was a very normal, good and decent Irish mother who never hesitated to bid the time of day, in contrast to the rest of the family. I read that Haughey's father had a record of service to our country and was a retired lieutenant. He was an invalid and though I passed his house daily for many years I never once saw the man. He may have been at home twenty four hours a day during which he may have put much thought into disciplining and 'bending the buds' to his liking and making Charley a man of steel with a brass neck.

It was strange that after asking neighbours what they thought of that family one usually got a frosty silence. Coonan said that the Haugheys were the kind who could not sit down to eat, unless they had a bunch of flowers on the table. What he meant I think was that they were full of pretence and sham but Charlie proved this to be wrong by his scholarly achievements. They were all very smart. Charlie's tremendous presence, at times as if he was on the way to bully someone, made him stand out among the crowd

Years later I heard that one of the Haugheys was a priest. I just could not believe it. I thought to myself that talent they had loads of, but virtue! The contradiction between Charlie's personality, his foul language his self agrandisment as people passed the gang at the corner and a priest in the family, implied a complete mystery to me (with the raw judgement of a teenager), because at that time we held priests in such reverence.

The only time I had any admiration for Charlie was when it appeared that he took a political risk in sending arms to the North, it humanized him to me for the first time. The most gut-wrenching tension I ever had , as a teenager and with the 'easily destructible' self assurance that went with it was when I was serving for a very short period with Charlie in the L.D.F. *(Local Defence Force)

Impertinence may serve a man in the army (probably the religious life as well). Somerset Maugham suggests that if one has two sons, one wild and the other quiet, the quiet one should go in the army as he would obey orders and get ahead and the wild one should join the religious life to get ahead.

During the emergency (better known as world war ll) many young men joined the Local Defence Force, a voluntary force formed to support the army in case the Germans or Brits invaded the country during the war. We were given a rifle and a uniform. On my first involvement Charlie (if my memory serves me) was in the regular uniform, the second time he was in an officer's uniform. This I would say was because of his educational background and rightly so. We did the usual marching and training and on one occasion it was decided to have a shooting contest. We were told to squeeze the trigger and to take a hair's breadth on the sights. We pooled in coins to make it more interesting for the winner. After winning the contest I had to sign with Charlie for the money as he was the officer in charge. As I did so, he was insolently silent until I regretted having won the contest. He could have said 'yer doin alright' or 'fuck you ye won', but a cutting silence was all I got which was mean.

Years later I was travelling to Los Angeles with Aer Lingus. Haughey had his fingers in the tax payer's pockets by commandeering the whole of the first class saloon for himself and his moth, (if one has power why not use it). I sat in the second aisle seat forward economy class. Suddenly to my astonishment, Charlie whipped open the curtain two metres away, looked me in the eyes, realized immediately who it was and hastily snapped the curtains closed.

The Haugheys while growing up were bad news for me. I was not as outgoing as I should have been, so there was no need to leave the L.D.F. because of Haughey causing some sleepless nights which I did.

I agree with Justice Minister Mary Harney when she says that Haughey should pay for his crimes. However it was that statement that got Charlie off the hook with the court. I am sceptical of her intentions considering her position and knowledge of the law. I believe her statement could have been self serving and political and should have been questioned in the Dail.

The Germans had a Ministry, The Ministry for *Propaganda*. The Brits called the same Ministry the Ministry for *Information* though in effect they both were the same. The Jerries would arrive as invaders while the Brits would arrive as saviours, though they would have been both equally welcome in our homestead. It was an anxious time, but we took comfort to note that Mr Hitler had no occupation plans for Ireland in his Mein Kampf. However I am digressing again and in the 'minds eye' Mrs Coonan, that lovely English neighbour, is frowning.

My sister (knitting fast enough even while she read) to have an unpleasant clicking sound knitted Bainin sweaters for each and every one of us. We wore them for fun while fitting our first gas mask and we looked like an Irish football team from Mars. It was a howl. Laughter was welcome and a 'life raft' during anxious times.

We had so many books that we had to convert and improve a 'fuel shed' to hold our library. There were books everywhere, on shelves in bookcases and stacked on the floor. A cousin after browsing through a book tossed it across the room disrespectfully on to a chair. My father became very upset and had little respect for the man ever after. Books were sacred in those days. The first thing that would catch our eye when we entered the house of a friend would be the books. They told where a man's heart was or his politics and were a sense of pride. Whenever I think back to the books, it creates the scenes and times in my memory more than anything else. The attitude towards life and reaction of each in the family to 'San Michele' for example was one of delight. I still have Epictetus by my bedside. Strange enough we did not have a bible in the house until the sixties when Monsignor Ronald Knox brought out a modern version.

Dad had a sideline when he retired which was reading for an organisation that examined books for submission to the literary censorship. He would arrive home with armfuls of books and read till his eyes grew tired and red with his pence nez glasses.. More than once he was late home after sitting through to the terminal bus stop, and finding himself on his way back into town still reading. We had an endless supply of books after father censored them of course. The ones he red-pencilled went to the high shelf! Once I fell off a chair while coursing through the pages. Later in 1968 a government censorship board was appointed, mostly run by retired people, who banned some of the classics of the 20th century like Ulysses. It was an over-reaction to consolidate our new independence. The church was the great educationalist and had a 'shout' in those days.

In the forties I attended Pembroke Technical schools to get a taste of various trades. After completing two years I set about finding a job. It was difficult to find one in those the worst of times. In August of 1948 my brother Malachi was in charge of security and fire at the airport and he suggested I take a job cleaning the aircraft and then try to get an apprenticeship in one of the workshops. After one week servicing the aircraft, I got work in the Radio Shop training as a Radio Mechanic. Two years down the log, I became a grade B Radio Mechanic with excellent pay. I loved Aer Lingus and we were proud of the company in those days, as if we owned it.

I spent many a weekend in Paris on the 'free' flights. Alas! I gave it all up to be with my girlfriend in London which was the worst mistake of my life. I must keep memories at bay at this point or I will digress. It happened unexpectedly, as love does sometimes, and at the worst possible time. I never got back in the trade until many years later when I went to sea.

CHAPTER FIVE

A smidgen of sadness

Monday morning, 30 March 1995

I took the eight o'clock train from Dublin to Portadown in the hope that a ninety eight year old man, named Robert Wright, who was born in the same neighbourhood as my father, could throw some light on father's younger years and help to furnish the missing years for the record.

He was thin as a whistle and walked upright with a cane to the parish church where my father was baptised. The church was surrounded by rough grass with some beer cans and a huge black ugly railing. The priest had just been on a 'sick call' and was tired, slightly abrupt and to the point he avowed, "There are no baptismal records because the church was set ablaze in the late eighteen hundreds by Loyalists and all the records were lost." I wished I had one member of the family with me and suddenly missed them. Communities marginalised in a never ending war

Thinking of father's troublesome youth, it occurred to me that he may have fooled the whole family and relatives for years and spent time in jail as a political prisoner and then decided to go to Dublin and simply would not talk about the past anymore. As Robert and I strolled to his house, he said, "I need a cup of coffee." "Isn't coffee bad for one?" I rambled, feeling a little foolish since he was ninety-six. His eyes were bright and his speech lucid enough, but even with the full volume on his hearing aid we still repeated everything three or four times. After an hour of shouting and trying to understand the Portadown accent, I felt a pressure on my arm from behind from his daughter who said he might be getting a little tired. I felt he could not be of any practical help, even if he had known father.

I realised how much he had been trying to help me and felt sorry for having stressed the old man. I apologised, thanked him and headed for the nearest restaurant where I had a hefty shepherd's pie, followed by hot apple tart and real cream, and of course, in those days no meal was complete without a cigarette and a cup of tay. Feeling bloated, I wondered why the French were so thin.

My job was just beginning. That was the only contact I had in the North at that time.

Two cousins named Lacy who lived in Belfast would take some time to locate so I decided first to go through the records of the various religious orders before tracking them down. I walked two miles in heavy weather and caught the Belfast-Dublin train, for Eastern Ireland and my home in beautiful Dalkey.

Miceal MacLiamor a noted actor of his day.

CHAPTER SIX

An Chronista

One of the nicest sounding words in the Irish language is *Chronista*. It is the name given to the one keeping the records in a church or monastery. The Reverend Stephen Redmond was the assistant Chronista for the Irish Jesuits in Glasnevan. While knocking on the door of his rectory early one morning in lamentable weather, a number of characters seemed to come from nowhere and gathered behind me looking for handouts. Casually dressed, I did not feel of smaller account sharing such company, far from it. For that matter, I have never had a passion as some people have to meet the celebrated. I prefer working folk who have character and are more real in their ways than people with money.

The door opened slowly to about six inches. A thin slightly bony ascetic face with a good smile, Father Stephen was greeted by a cloud of cigarette smoke and body odour sucked in the door and a hearty 'good morning father' by all. He knew them on sight. He told a young able-bodied man that he was not going to help him today. The man grew red, stared, as if the priest owed him, then walked away fuming, looking forward I guess to a dull dry day.

Father Stephen bid me pass into a room which had an uninviting dusty silence about it. I sought a period in my father's life that could have been a black spot. A little apprehensive that I might be inviting a sermon about minding my own business and leaving 'well enough' alone, my mind became hyperactive.

Life is a mystery, life is really a mystery. We know nothing and we can know nothing. If the brain is a muscle then point to the mind. Where is the mind, point to it. The brain is the hurling stick and *'I'm the sliotar'*. Oh for a day back in California, I thought, with our "Ping Pong have a nice day" culture where hardly a serious thought could ruin my day or furrow my brow. I thought about the eleven years in father's history that was missing. My father, possibly sick of children at school and at home, probably almost expired when mother, after six kids, enlightened him that she was pregnant at fifty.

I loved to go out with father. Once, when I was about four years and on the way to the Eye and Ear hospital, we stopped at Liberty Hall and visited big Jim Larkin, the Union leader. Big Jim was delighted to meet Patrick Joseph Segundo (as he called me) and patted me on the head. Eyes sparkling, he took me on his bony knee. Even at age four, I surmised he was a man different and charismatic. I was on his knee for what seemed a long, uneasy time and began feeling cold. On the way out of Liberty Hall I heard a jingle and found coins in my pocket! Alfey Burn crossed the road to shake hands as he often did with people. A young past pupil stopped us and asked if Dad knew where he could get a job.

So were my thoughts sitting in the rectory when in walked Father Stephen for whom I was waiting, apologising for the delay. This saintly man, a Companion of Jesus, had spent fourteen years studying philosophy, theology, and very likely Psychology and law and here he was spending his morning dealing handouts to the deservedly poor, along with cadgers. The Jesuits founded the great universities and hospices of Europe. Whether I thought it futile or not, credit goes to the Jesuit because 'his compass always pointed to charity' which is what Christianity is all about!

I told him the story of the missing eleven years in father's life, and the years over which a pall was drawn. "Strange! Very strange" he said becoming interested. "I will be happy to check the records and get back to you in a week or ten days. Invariably for some strange reason, if so and so was a religious and little is known about him or his whereabouts, he must surely have been a Jesuit". He smiled.

Americans were piling out of buses a week later, as Fr Stephan and my brother Kevin and I walked into Jury's Hotel for lunch. He wore his clerical garb, a rare thing to do in the year 2000. I ordered cod fish with colcannon and parsnips, Kevin and his reverence asked for grilled salmon and sprouts. The priest was viewed with great esteem by the waitresses, who surprisingly already knew him. They became very gay and chatty.

The time for news or a gift is after ordering a good meal. When the waitresses left, Father removed his glasses and said "I have disappointing news: *I could not find any record of your father being in the seminary.*"

He handed me a list of areas where I might continue my search, and gave me support and encouragement. My brother, Kevin (with a humour so dry it squeaked) was so enchanted with the company it took us two hours to finish the meal. He was surprised at what I was doing and pleased about it, to my great relief. He suggested that he, my sister and I should get together and recall what we knew about Father and our relatives.

I was disappointed and puzzled at the lack of any record, since mother mentioned the Jesuits. The next day I headed for Maynooth College. That great generation station of Irish Catholic priesthood that seemed proud to make a distinction, in the old days, between an 'Irish Catholic' and a 'Roman Catholic' because when we put our minds to it we Irish do better, I thought.

As I was on the way to Maynooth, I passed St. Patrick's Cathedral. The last time I had been there or even seen it was when our teacher in the primary school had taken the class to visit it as part of a history lesson. Now I was so impressed with the exterior I got out of the car and had a strange feeling that I was indeed on holy ground, as one might be at a shrine. I quickly 'lost altitude' however upon entering the building!

The original site was marked out by St. Patrick himself as an ideal location for a church. The present Cathedral is built on the site of a very old previous church. There was a notice on the door saying that this was *The Church of Ireland Cathedral* (quite a claim) and that there was an entrance fee. I paid something like five dollars, with the puerile thought that one did not pay to mount the hill of Calvary. Years ago mother would have turned pale at the thought of entering a Protestant church, I kidded myself that now I had the answer!

The Cathedral was full of non-religious historical figures. A statue of a bald headed Saint Anthony would be entirely out of place here, so it has been out of fashion in the Church of Ireland. In fact even one of Saint Patrick (with his foot on a snake) himself would seem out of place. Looking upward toward the roof there was a Roman Forum effect from all the flags. The faded dusty streamers were there to honour achievements to the 'killing trades' of Britain. No validity, a nasty hiccup in the history of the site.

I soon lost interest, walked across to Francis Street and entered 'The Old Dublin' restaurant. where I ate *'Dublin coddle' washed down by a pint of Guinness, followed by a blanc-mange, a cup of tea and a fag though now I am a fanatic against smoking. Feeling good after a wholesome meal I left the restaurant, looked across the street at the massive Cathedral, and regretted not spending more time there and decided to return another day, because, the place was log-jammed with history.

So on to Maynooth, to that magnificent complex of buildings - architectural gems! Maynooth is an historic town, though in County Kildare it is only twenty-four kilometres west of Dublin. It has a fine castle built in 1203 and a manorial church which was 'incorporated' into the Church of Ireland. Maynooth's seminary is the largest on the islands of Ireland and Britain and one of the most famous in the world.

I went to the information desk. A slim young man named Donal, with long curly dark hair, bright blue eyes and a smile showing that goodness and courtesy was naturel to him, offered to assist me. I asked if a P.J. Quinn had ever studied for the priesthood there. He took a journal from under the counter, browsed through it and informed me right away, as if he were checking a nightly hotel register, that there was no record of a P.J. Quinn from Portadown having studied there.

So simple, I could have just phoned. I expected a trip to the archives and a chat with the chronista. I shrugged. "Go to Armagh, Ulster, which has primal authority over church records in Ireland," he urged. I decided on the way home to have lunch with my brother and sister as soon as possible..

*Dublin coddle is an old Dublin dish consisting of onions, potatoes, pork sausages, streaky bacon, parsley and stock.

CHAPTER SEVEN

Eva, my sister the nun, friend and my delight.

"The time has come" the Walrus said
"To talk of many things"   Alice in wonderland

My sister Eva (eighty one years old, ex-Principal of Dunmanway College of Domestic Science in County Cork) who is totally deaf in one ear and has poor hearing in the other, a brother Kevin of seventy five years who cannot hear himself bark and with a dry cough that would crack a Guinness glass, (a trait that appeared over and over in the family), my sister Sheila and I, both mobile and in good health, we all entered Finnegan's Pub on the Sorrento Road in Dalkey for lunch.

We dared not tell her she was going to a pub until we wheeled her chair in while her jaw fell. She had never eaten, (as far as I knew) in a pub. "Aren't those lovely table settings," she said to our relief. She had a ferocious appetite. No matter how good the meal, she always insisted that it was not complete without a bottle of Pommard or Beaujolais wine. Not any particular cheese, but a selection of cheeses to finish with, well aware who was paying the tag, summoning the waiter as if he were for her alone.

My brother (while putting the waiter on notice after a sharp cough), recalled in a serious mood, "I can't understand why the Jesuits have no record, can you explain it Eva?" "Well perhaps Paddy gave them the wrong dates," (putting me in my place; she set the status for everyone in the family). I ignored the remark.

"The curious thing about my father" said Kevin "in all my years living with him he never once talked about religion. He never asked were you at Mass this week."

"Did he ever discuss religion in the family?" I asked while Kevin mused as if to make sure he was right. Eva intimated.

"No never".

Here we were dining in Finnegan's pub/restaurant, on a gloomy winter's day; reiterating, that Father, a man with a family of nine practising Catholics; never once discussed religion with us, even though he went weekly to church and was himself an schoolmaster. God! What kind of a family are we that the idea of talking about religion or the very thought of praying together seemed taboo in a Catholic household? Did going to mass gave us all the parts of the bible we needed to know?

"And why was that Eva?" prodded Kevin.

"It is a curious thing about the man indeed!" Eva confirmed.

"If he was in the religious life and later opted out, was he leaving his religion behind him, pushing it aside? But why could he never talk about it!"

"You know he really was a member of the Jesuit community in Rathfarnham and frequently returned there for Retreats," said Eva.

There was a pause and then Kevin, who seemed to be tired of the subject, having had it all his life, said

"There is another thing, the same thing again, what you-may-call him, Jim McGrath mother's brother, came to Dublin. Our mother and father lived in 10 Ring Street, Inchicore with seven children, in two tiny bedrooms and they took him in. How in heaven did they manage? The British military were regularly raiding houses, but they invariably marked an X on our door! Once they burst in and while searching the various rooms, mother stood erect concealing her brother's pistol under her skirt!"

The waiter placed the food with separate plates for the vegetables. I felt a little apprehensive when he filled the few vacant spots on the small bar table, with tall wine glasses, because Eva was within arms length and winding herself up. I could see her decking the tall glass of wine.

"And there is no trace of Uncles and Aunts apart from the Mother Superior in Seville and Peadar in Scotland, both now dead?", I asked. "He never used to talk about his family, ever ever," Eva remonstrated.

"When Uncle Peadar died, in May 1929, we were old enough to attend his funeral in Glasgow yet father never said a word. This would have been an opportunity to meet the relations" retorted Kevin. "There were two sisters, relations of mother, Minnie and Madge who lived only a few miles from each other, yet Minnie didn't know for years that Madge had married," recalled Kevin.

"The whole thing is a complete mystery and it's dangerous too I think. The sad thing about it is nobody's alive to unravel the mystery," Eva pondered. Sheila was unusually quiet. She poured the wine.

"Do you remember our first birthday party?" I asked Sheila in a lighter mood more to get our minds on the mechanics of eating.

"There was never a birthday party," said Sheila. I was so engrossed in thought that I overturned a glass of wine which was quickly mopped by the waiter.

"You must have had a birthday party, Janey Mack! Someone must have said 'happy birthday' so what did happen on your birthday?" I interjected.

"How did you celebrate it?"

"We didn't, there were times when my birthday came and went and not one even remembered it!" Kevin mused.

"In those days there was no such a thing as a birthday party, people didn't bother. There were problems and life wasn't easy or simple. Your birthday party was merely your Sunday dinner. Partying wasn't affordable or fashionable. But there was a wonderful spirit of sharing and helping the less fortunate survive in decency with a modicum of comfort," explained Eva and nicely I thought.

Time after time we remembered that Father never talked about his family nor left any details. The family never got to know relations. From the turn of the century to the fifties, probably still over-reacting to the Reformation, men and women of Ireland entered the priesthood and nunneries in large numbers, building a spiritual empire, such as we had done centuries before, when this country was known as the land of Saints and Scholars. With this thought I picked up the tab, paid the tariff and we parted..
.

It was not uncommon, from the turn of the century, to have a whole family enter the Church. It may have been that the evil seen during five revolutions in two hundred years and war drove people searching for a better world. Something had to be done to kill the hatred.

In France there was a surge of vocations after the war. One most notable, a famous Count, gave away a fortune when his wife became a nun and he a priest. In Germany, Goethe's grandson became a Jesuit and in America, Dulles son a Presbyterian converted and became a priest. He is now a Cardinal. Maynooth's wall-to-wall display of photos gives ample evidence of this.

The reason for my father's reluctance to talk about his family was probably that, out of a family of thirteen, all but two may have entered the religious life. Mother has mentioned that he did something which in his time was unheard of and somewhat shameful! The day before his ordination he left! But why was there no record? Why, if he spent five (or whatever) years in a Jesuits novitiate is there no information of any kind? It is bizarre. We, his family, believe there are many questions to be answered. Did he leave for the patriot aim, to join the I. R. B? We remain 'in the dark' about some eleven years of P.J's life and, as a result, don't know the whereabouts of the Quinn dynasty. There were twenty-nine Secular priests ordained in Armagh during a period when any one of them could have been a relative Quinn!

My mother as I knew her would be a strange person to the women of today. She came from a farm. Farmers lived with a lot of fear in earlier days. They were afraid the weather might fail, afraid of being evicted, afraid of the government, calving, even of an eccentric priest. Mother had *fears from childhood* but was completely unafraid when it came to the *fears of adulthood*. I saw her turn pale while we got her to peep in the entrance to a Protestant church. She talked about the English King Henry about Elizabeth cutting off Catholic Mary's head, the great division they caused in the church. "*No I won't put my foot inside*". She said.

She would prefer to miss a tram than ride on the upper deck and the idea of flying was unnatural. Worst of all, she could never pick up a telephone. My nephew had installed a phone (a rare thing in the fifties). He handed it suddenly to her one evening and said, "Paddy is on the phone from Quebec." She would not take the phone, he held it to her ear and I shouted, "Say something Ma, do you hear me, its Paddy calling from Quebec." I knew she wanted to talk to me as much as I wanted to talk to her. I had paid nine dollars a minute and felt sad, in fact devastated for some time afterwards. I thought I was going to make her happy and only frightened her. She could navigate through a flood of traffic after making the sign of the cross, dragging me across O'Connell Street but she was still living in the eighteen hundreds when it came to a phone.

I was thirty seven at the time, a bored clerk (pencil on the ear) when I tried my first shot at reporting with an article about a house in which Thomas Moore stayed and wrote his poem:-

'Row Brothers row the tide runs fast, the rapids are near and the daylights past

Sing to Saint Andrew a parting hymn, Row Brothers row the light grows dim'

It was about a beautiful old house on the banks of the Saint Lawrence River. I sent the article, along with a photograph of the owner, Jesse MacDonald, to the Irish Independent. It was an appeal to Ireland not to let the house be demolished. I had completely forgotten about it when three weeks later, there arrived a cutting from the Irish Independent newspaper, with a letter from Ma with the notation. "There is more than one Paddy Quinn in Quebec." She did not know I had written the article but connected me with it, which seemed more than a coincidence and strange. She felt I would be interested in it. I replied, "No, Ma, there is only yours truly in Quebec, and he has become a handy man with the pen". About six weeks later I received a welcome cheque from the newspaper. Many times while in London she instinctively knew if I was sick or troubled and got in touch.

My father was the personification of Nationalist Ireland and worked all his life to that end. He knew when the heart spoke, when it came to justice. He knew the goodness an angry man can carry and how close a profaner could be to Jesus. He spoke frankly and was not afraid of displeasing any man in the Dail or on the streets. When I would run into the hooks and twists of the law later in California I could not help but notice the sham and recognise the distrust people have there in getting justice. I have nothing but disdain for a system that can let a murderer like O.J. run free and mistakenly send innocent men to the chair.

It was a memorable lunch and having jogged on so far with this 'matter of fact' serious material, I hope the reader does not think that life was absurd for us as a family. Life was strange and difficult during the 'troubles' and I stand by the veracity of things as I saw them. We were in truth a happy a family.

I never discovered the truth about the missing eleven years of my father's life. It remains a mystery, one that perhaps may never be unravelled. He was 57 when I was born and it's a sad fact that most of the people who might be able to help explain the missing years are now dead. Some day I might discover the real story. However, life goes on and I had my own difficulties and experiences to come to terms with.

CHAPTER EIGHT

London

In August 1948, I went to London and after a month in a boarding house near Victoria Station, I was accepted into a residence similar to the Y.M.C.A. which catered mostly for students. I had a room mate who loved to play the violin which was the only time we spent together except for an occasional breakfast in the dining hall as he was a busy student and had a girlfriend.

One evening in the second week, I was on my way home after buying a new pair of shoes, when I was called aside by two men in civilian clothes. They told me they were police and snatched the box from my hand. After examining the contents and a quick swipe to see if I had a weapon they let me go. Why was I suspect? The day before I asked directions, to be told; "by the way you'll pass a Post Office in case you wish to blow it up". It was a joke of course. I returned to the hostel and made a mistake in telling my roommate what had happened. The net result was that I sensed a cloud of suspicion in the game room and elsewhere that was difficult to handle or much less understand. I felt distant from the populace as if they were from Timbuktu . Casually people called me Paddy and when they asked my real name it usually drew a smile or a laugh when I said Paddy.

I needed to find people who thought the same and spoke with my own tongue. The Pub gave a sense of community and was the only place one could feel secure and safe at least for a short while. As time went by my income increased and I rented a one bed-roomed flat on Cromwell road in the Royal Borough of Kensington owned by an Irish family. The pavements were still pockmarked from explosion splashes; iron gates and railings that were taken for the war effort, left houses with an unfinished appearance. Memories of our neutrality were still fresh.. Shops at Earls Court, where I lived, advertised flats to rent with the tag '*no Irish need apply*'.

When the Irish born Jewish Duke of Wellington returned to Ireland after the battle of Waterloo, he ran for a seat in Parliament, hoping that the

Irish would all rush to vote for him after his great victory against Napoleon. He was disappointed at the few votes he got and made a sour grapes statement "being born in a stable does not make one a horse". Strangely Churchill had a similar experience after the war and lost out to the labour party. People needed leaders who would give them work and were probably afraid Churchill might sit on his laurels. Unemployment was high.

St Albans was a lovely old roman city surrounded by green fields, north of London. One day, while on a visit there, I met some Ukrainians who invited me to play tennis in the grounds of St. Alban's mental hospital. I was impressed by their work and thought it would be interesting I took a 'bridge' job in the hospital as a trainee nurse. I wanted to help those put away to hear their stories or talk to them.   I studied mental stress and being somewhat stressed myself at that time, found friendship and understanding there. The affect a book titled "Be glad you are neurotic" my first book on psychology, had on me was indeed a valuable read, and put me at ease with life as no other book has ever done since.

I was given a uniform and 'full board''. I was apprehensive about taking the job for more reasons than one, jobs were few and the need was there to survive. We had good food and recreation facilities and my main distraction were ping pong and tennis which we played daily. Our first two weeks training was given by a nurse from Galway to a class half-Irish and the rest Ukrainians and Poles. We were taught Grey's Anatomy, bandaging and day to day care of the insane, such as giving enemas and shaving them and giving them medicine and how to secure it in the cabinets.

There is not a nobler calling than nursing to those who are suited to it. After a few weeks I was asked to assist at a lobotomy operation

The dictionary states lobotomy is 'the surgical cutting into or across the lobe of the brain for the treatment of mental disorders'. It is not a simple everyday procedure. It troubled me long after I left the hospital and still feel it was the wrong thing to do to any human being. it is a ghastly thing to do in fact.

During the 1914-1918 war it was found that soldiers, who had bayonets thrust through the skull and brain and recovered, underwent a change of personality. The aggressive became the timid and vice versa. Why not instead of a bayonet use a chisel on mental patients, move the brain around and see if they might react more normally. They did, that was how lobotomy came into being and that is why it is practised today, assuming it is still performed.

One muggy Monday morning we (four male nurses) brought a patient to the operating room a handsome strong young Pole in his thirties; a noisy and difficult patient, who sometimes spent days in the padded cell. He had been an officer in the Polish London - based army. We fastened a belt, with built in handcuffs, around his waist and manacled his wrists.We put foot irons with about a foot of chain around his ankles. We struggled got him on the trolley and strapped him down while he sweated and roared oaths in Polish. I clearly recall the man's face as I write because it was indeed a sad case. He was once a man of authority and education before going insane.

The surgery the doctor performed was to lift the eyelid, hammer a chisel through the skull into the brain and then move the brain around with the chisel. He pulled out the chisel, lifted the other eyelid and went through the same procedure. We wheeled the man out of the theatre, his eyes black and blue. The treatment of the mentally ill with the use of lobotomy and shock treatment (sending an electric shock through the head) is cruel and unusual punishment. It is forbidden by the Eight Amendment and should be punishable by law.

An hour after the operation, while putting a coin in the nickelodeon during lunch, a male nurse told me that I looked pale. I responded with a question to avoid discussing the surgery.

"Do you want to go to the films later?"

"Sure," he replied

"What's on?"

"I don't know, but we should get moving, it's late."

We arrived at the theatre, entered and sat down to relax, not knowing or caring what was on. Then after the advertisements came 'Presenting Alfred Hitchcock's Psycho'. God, didn't we have enough of this, I fumed. My mate, exasperated, sank down in his seat as if to go asleep. What a day of days, I lamented. I decided on the way home from the film, that I did not have the right 'stuff' for life at St. Albans. My brain was too active and I found it hard to slow it down at times. I was too impersonal to be efficient.

During my time in London I studied watercolour painting and worked with the Legion of Mary. Loneliness had become a serious problem and it was causing depression. I found myself at times frightened by my own solitude. While reaching out to others in the Pub, having the 'craic' and belly laughs was great while it lasted, but didn't help after I turned the key in my flat. I tried the 'less travelled road' which was giving time to the Legion of Mary and in doing good I learned a lot about myself and learned to handle time better and found a higher aim, (even though my shot was very weak), that of eternity.

Members were mostly Polish, Spanish and Irish in our presidium. We went house to house, 'cap in hand' bearing back from the door rather than having the foot in the door and answering questions about the Catholic Church.

"Why do Catholics behave well and go to church on Sunday but are bad the rest of the week?"

"It's better to be good *one* day of the week than bad the whole seven!" My answers were raw and inexperienced to begin with.

The President of the 'Queen of the Angels' Presidium in the rich borough of Knightsbridge was a tall blond Englishman named Bailey. He was a wealthy entrepreneur, cultured and polite, who had converted from the Anglican Church. He was well read and owned bookshops in the west end of London. The vice President, who owned a factory in London, impressed me by his experiences in overcoming temptations in the Middle East during the war. He succeeded in being faithful to his wife by saying the rosary. He said he loved her and looked one straight in the eye in a way that one knew he was telling the truth.

I felt stronger spiritually with both of these good Englishmen and it helped me live a clean life. The strange thing about Bailey was that no matter how often I tried to discuss the convert Cardinal Newman's 'Apolgia', he cautioned me not to. The book he said was not good for non-Catholics and confused 'would be' Catholics! I never could see why. He took me on my first door to door visit as if training for a job. We made notes for a full recall, so that the next person to go to the door, would know where we left off and how the people felt about the church or if they were in need of physical help.

Once we were having a long argument with a very smart lapsed catholic who was a Communist. The party was making great headway at that time. "Religion is the opiate of the people; the church is the poor man's opera; all wars are caused by religion". He argued like the Devil himself but Bailey's reasoning powers were so remarkable that they left my jaw hanging in a stupor. I have forgotten most men I met, but remember everything about Brother Bailey. There is no one I would rather be with, or dare to contradict, than this man while discussing the church. He seemed to know what one was thinking before the mouth was opened. I was amazed at the knowledge and intelligence Bailey intimated at every door. He had all the answers and I greatly profited from listening to him. He respected my opinion and helped me communicate. The communist, angry at losing the argument, told us that we were insane. Bailey, in his relaxed slow way, sarcastically asked

"Do you have a diploma in psychiatry?" I smothered a laugh. Of course we were not there to win arguments, by doing so one would be likely to lose a soul we were told, but to help remove ignorance about the church and keep people informed. As we walked away, his wife suddenly appeared laughing and seemed delighted someone stood up to her husband and, with a north of England accent, insisted that we come in for a cup of tea. We talked about the man's hobby which was building small boats and then magically putting them into bottles. I guessed he may have been a seaman.

I noticed his wife from time to time at the church. My door to door answers were not academic like Baileys but I was a good listener. We reported all involvements to the Presidium, where they were recorded. especially the needs, material or spiritual, of those contacted.

There were happy times in London with sweetness and delights. Good theatre, concerts in the Albert Hall when one could afford them and foreign movies. The Bunch of Grapes pub ('Vatican Arms') after one o'clock mass opposite the Brompton Oratory where we gassed up for 'Spouters' Corner' (Hyde Park Corner) became a routine.

Spirituality in those days was a source of strength and joy for the masses. Legion duty was an hour during the week for the Lord, which helped us walk with Him the rest of the workdays. It was at a later meeting of the same Legion of Mary years later, that I met my wife, Myriam Sanchez, in Los Angeles.

Yet for thirteen years I had an unproductive unfocused time changing jobs and drinking. At an Irish dance in Kilburn or Hammersmith, I have forgotten which one, I got in conversation with a couple who were going to Canada on a government supported scheme.

In 1957 during the Suez 'crisis', Canada encouraged immigration by paying the fare across the Atlantic on condition it would be paid back in two years. Within the month I sailed on a Greek ship. It could handle more human cargo which seemed in the thousands cheaply than other lines. Some slept on hampers.

I went to Montreal which, along with Buenos Aires, is one of the two most 'European' cities in the Americas.

CHAPTER NINE

Canada

Iscarcely know how to describe the first aspect of a country so different to Ireland and strange in forms and customs and language. It was not too long after the war, feelings were still high, so I conceived it would be easier to make friends in French speaking Quebec (which, like Ireland, for the most part wanted to remain neutral, but was forced into the war). I chose to live in Quebec because it was Catholic. I found the culture and the language interesting, though tiring to begin with and hard to grasp the first few months.

The utterance of such sentiments now, I know, would be inconceivable. However after living in London soon after the war and, because Ireland remained neutral I found bigotry and circumstances there which not a little augmented my disinclination to live west of Quebec. There was little fraternity between the French and English speaking areas of Canada at that time and a strong movement for separation. If there was going to be trouble, I would be more sympathetic to our ancient allies the French in those difficult fifties. A war between the Brits and the Egyptians was raging. Anthony Eden, the Prime Minister of England said "we are not at war with Egypt only in armed conflict". Can anyone read the Lion's eyes or understand British politicians? De Gaulle's 'Quebec Libre' statement gave me goose pimples and shook Canada to its bones.

The Canadian weather can go from eighty degrees in Montreal in the summer to forty below in the winter. *Dublin is further north but much warmer. I spent my first two years in mid Canada on a Royal Canadian air force base, during the cold war. There were two 'distant early warning systems', the DEW Line and the Mid Canada line, which were radars focused towards Russia running across Canada under the American air force authority, It would give a warning should Russia attack across Canada. It cost many billions of dollars to run and install.

Two weeks after I arrived in Montreal, I was trying to order a hamburger in Kresge's store. "Je desire un hamburger et chips, s'il vous plait" I said (trying to remember Moran's French Grammar).

"Un Hamburger et des frites, monsieur?"

" Des frites, que es que sait? French Fry? Hamburger and chips, Madame!"

"Oui, des frites! des frites. Je comprend, monsieur!" said the teen blond counter girl

"Chips are called des Frites in French", said a slightly heavy set lady sitting beside me at the counter.

The woman introduced herself as Mary Murphy. I told her I was new to Canada and was looking for work. She happened to be a personnel officer for the Bell Telephone company and within the week thanks to her I had a remunerative job.

I was on a plane heading for the 'Distant Early Warning' line in the north and a job that I would be in for two years, which was a long time to suffer the cruellest of climates and deprivation. That was a stroke of luck that gave me a bank account and security I had never before experienced. We signed on for six months at a time and could not leave before the time was up.

After a security check which took about a week, we flew north in a military DC8 cargo plane (mostly beer, the water was lousy) to the Royal Canadian Air Force Base near Great Whale river, on the Hudson Bay. If the snow leaves for the banquet of summer, it returns sometimes in weeks. The base was comfortable, we each had our own room and the food was excellent. I had a simple duty in the store and if anything didn't have quite enough to do. Strangely the biggest danger was walking from the bar to the quarters, a ten minute walk. Two men were lost from hypothermia, (which took less than ten minutes to kill) after falling in the snow while walking from the bar to the camp.

One morning I went cross country on skies, (which is slow going on flat snow. I never got used to snow shoes) to an Eskimo village igloo to which I had been directed to enquire about fishing on the bay. There was a light fog and I could smell the camp before it came into view. Huskies, always hungry and tied to stakes, jumped wild and howled as I approached. Noisy seabirds of many kinds with cantankerous sounds reconnoitred for garbage. Disappointed they flew up and down attacking each other. After the lonely, quiet cross country, the stillness was shattered as the noise became louder and louder until the whole area vibrated to the sound of the dog's howling and the birds' loud cries, before the birds flew towards the bay joining the geese and ducks flying low along the Hudson shoreline.

The racket turned the whole village out at seven o'clock in the morning. Eskimos, surprised to see someone so early, beckoned me in. Even though the temperature was below freezing the igloo was warm and cosy I left my skis and poles outside the igloo, which was a regrettable mistake because a Husky dog which got loose ate the leather straps but was considerate enough to leave the poles. As I was overwhelmed with the odour from the igloo after a large breakfast, I hesitated, gestured that I wanted to go fishing rather than eat. The man understood and told me to wait while he prepared the kayak and fishing gear. He asked for twenty dollars which at the time was an outrageous sum. I understood because they in turn were ripped off by the Hudson Bay Company, which was the only market for hundreds of miles.

The word Eskimo is an Indian word meaning raw flesh eater (That is why there is a tendency now to drop the word and use Inuit). The Indians cook their meat. My first introduction to eating raw flesh was on a Sunday afternoon's walk with an Italian priest named Fr. Rockler O.M.I. We were climbing a hill when Father's eye fell on a flat stone; similar to the ones we would use skimming the sea in Clontarf as kids. He aimed at a bird in a small dead bush and felled it in the first try. I was beside myself for a moment at the priest being so cruel, but held my silence as was customary when a priest did something wrong.

He plucked the young bird (which was the size of a sparrow), tore a leg of and ate it. "It's good!" he hastened to say, "Here try the other leg!" I looked at the tiny leg, hesitated a moment. "So small it can't harm, I guess Cheers!" Consenting, I bit into the flesh. "Yes it is good, isn't it, and tastes like fish?" I assented cautiously, looking at the remains in his hand. That was the first time I ate Sushi (in California the word Sushi is not just applied to fish) and have enjoyed many a good meal of raw flesh in Japanese restaurants since. According to the lifeboat directions on survival which were on our ships, there is no animal on earth that one can't eat raw and there are only three fish that can kill, one being the bubble fish.

To return to the village, the Eskimo and I dragged the kayak to the water rim. I paddled on one side at the stern and he sat up front over the bow, gazing into the water with a spear and fishing line. The early morning fog grew denser so we could only hear the flocks of geese as they passed overhead. There was a growing rapid ripple on the water vibrating the kayak from bow to stern. After about twenty minutes "Inuk" (the man) pulled a big tomcod fish from the water, turned to me waving it triumphantly. If it hadn't been for the ripple nauseating me I might have cheered. He then took a knife from his belt, cut the fish's belly from head to tail, ran his finger through the fish scooping up the whole inners (which we would dispose of in the garbage) and downed the lot thereon! I involuntarily evacuated my breakfast over the side and perhaps more and left Inuk to do the paddling.

On the way from the village to the base I ran into fog. It was worrying without the straps on my poles. Dropping one pole I reached over too far and slid off the hard path because of poor visibility while picking it up and fell into six feet of fluffy snow. One ski came off in the fall. Half lying, half standing I removed a glove but the metal strap 'burned' the skin instantly (as it was about 40 degrees below) and I had to replace the glove. I looked to the sky, taking a bearing on the hard surface, then, holding the loose ski vertical, climbed upon it and threw myself to the side towards the path and managed to crawl by raising myself on the ski to the hard surface. I must have been under snow for four terrifying minutes which was the most fearful experience in my life...

It was now afternoon and the fog had lifted. The sky was red above and the wind was in a southerly direction. I looked forward to spring, when the rising temperature melted the frozen branches while small delicate buds ventured out, a happy change from the cruel winter.

In the distance I saw a group of Eskimos assembling near the bay, busy beaching a seal. Safe again, I breathed deeply, paused awhile and then headed for the gathering. As I got closer I could see the Inuit cutting and pulling pieces from a big seal to eat. When on the water seals are greatly feared by the Eskimos just as they are by fishermen in small boats in California were the men (illegally) carry pistols to shoot them. While a man's back is turned a seal will jump into a kayak or small wooden boat, grab a fish and in so doing overturn the boat. Many an Eskimo has been killed this way

I reached for my camera and walked over to the crowd but the women shooed me away. They did not like being photographed while their hands were red with blood from the raw seal and the blood was dripping down their coverings. I understood and put the camera away.

A man invited me to have some flesh. I noticed that the seal's eyes were missing and most of the hind quarters. I wondered if the eyes were a delicacy like those of the caribou. When a caribou is killed the first thing eaten are the eyes and then the undigested food in the belly is cut out and eaten. If a piece of raw seal was dished up Japanese style in a restaurant along with rice and sauce I would enjoy it, as many do the world over, but because of the sea smell of the seal and the odour of the company, though hungry, I declined, hoping I had not made any ill feelings.

As I was leaving a man shouted while pointing to the bay and cried "Aurrit aurrit-walrus!", I halted, scanned the bay and in the distance about five hundred metres away, I saw on a block of slow moving ice a large walrus basking in the brilliant afternoon sun. It was a most unusual occurance. The men unbelieving this gift from heaven darted to the kayaks, floated them and paddled towards the Walrus. One kayak was ahead of the rest. It slowed as it came near the floating ice, so as not to disturb the animal Walruses will let one come almost within touching distance before deciding to move or stay put. Many a man has been killed when they overturned the kayak and threw them into the freezing water. A cormorant landed beside the Walrus as a companion. The walrus lifted its head, looked around ignoring the bird and then quietly lay back again as the lone kayak cautiously stopped, then moved slowly and quietly towards the animal. If this had been a seal then –flip and down under for twenty minutes, which is their maximum under water before they have to come up for air. At a close distance the Inuit on his knees launched a deadly blow with his spear. Instantly the other kayaks speeded to finish the kill and secure the walrus. It was hard paddling before they got the Walrus over the driftwood and on to the beach.

There was great excitement on the shore by the women because now they not only had good food in plenty but with the blubber they could mix in some other substance (memory fails me here) and they would have oil for the lamps to light and to heat the igloo. As the men paddled back to shore against the wind and manoeuvring the walrus, some lost their caps. The walrus was heavy and the paddling like a marathon. The women meanwhile busied themselves hanging the remains of the seal to dry in the sun. The bladder was kept for 'show off purposes' at ceilies (gatherings).

The walrus beached, the Inuit who had thrust the first spear walked proud. The skin was his and he began skinning the walrus before sharing the remains with the others. His wife would have her work 'cut out' for her making Mukluks (seaskin boot) and other garments. The skin would be split in two and used to cover their oomiaks (Curraghs). It had many uses such as small net ropes and laces. For clothing and bedding it would have to be stretched and dried. When an Oogruk was killed, the windpipe was used for soft leather purposes and the stomach prepared and made into containers.

The Eskimos have to speak with much feeling because such words as 'excuse me' or 'please' don't exist in their language, neither does the word love. For the latter they say "let's laugh a little" which is fitting because one usually laughs at the ridiculous positions while doing it. As far as I know they do not have an alphabet or written language although I heard that there was an O.M.I. priest working on producing one for them.

The wind was now coming from the North there were grey spots on the sky and a heavy ripple in the sea. A pale greenish white light was dancing on and off about the sky, Moving slowly, I walked from the beach on the skies until I got to the snow and then skied fast to get to the base before sundown. My legs were tired and I had bleeding shins from the fall. The sun had set by the time I got to the base and, strangely, my arrival is very vivid in my memory, perhaps because of the strange day.

I was famished and had two medium rare steaks at the canteen with Fr Rockler and some friends.

"Good isn't it," I said.

"Yes but you've spoiled it with all that H.P. sauce", said the priest.

I surmised that if the priest had been in the village, he would have had to join the happy feast. I am sure he has already done so many times for the cause he had at heart, as well as the food. He told us that one time while he was eating seal the daughter of a woman being bashful with him, said,

"I hate these greasy hands and chins covered with blood."

The mother replied,

"Daughter, do not worry about what's on the outside of the body that can be washed clean. It is the dirt or decay that is collected in the soul that one should be concerned about". If memory serves me right there is a similar statement in the Bible.

"I'm going to the Indian village tomorrow," said Rockler.

"With a dog sledge" I queried.

"Yes! After the eleven o'clock mass for a baptism! Would anyone like to come? It will be the last chance of a sledge ride because the Eskimos are heading north."

There was a knock at the canteen window behind us. An Eskimo wanted to make sure we needed the dogs. No one volunteered, Father turned to me as I was the only Catholic at the table, "O.K" I said reluctantly feeling dead tired.

The following day it was almost two p.m. before we donned our parkas and left the base to pick up the sledge (which was twelve feet long and four feet wide) to drive to the Indian village. Innuk was hitching the dog lines to the sledge as we arrived at the Eskimo's tent,. "Quick get on the sledge fast" said father. He knew that once the eleven dogs felt they were hitched to the sledge they would take off and we might not be able to leap on. Father (who spoke Eskimo) took the reins, cried Haru Haru (go left) to the dogs and put us in the direction of the Indian village while cracking the whip picking up speed..

The dogs were half wild and were kept tied to stakes when not working. They are kept hungry enough to want to work and howl a lot from hunger and while being fed. Domestic dogs should be fed after the family have eaten to show who is boss or 'lead dog' so as they become obedient. Eskimo dogs on the other hand are always fed first starting with the lead dog and working down. This is to flatter their survival instincts and stave off an attack by putting Innuk low in the line of the dog dynasty. Innuk cannot see a man or an animal sometimes a few meters away in a snowstorm but the dogs can smell one and lead the way as far as a kilometer. They can also smell the salt sea water and they turn away if the ice is getting dangerously thin. The dogs decide by fighting who the lead is going to be. They don't always fight fair and can cunningly, after a long time plotting, gang up on a lead dog if he was vicious with them.

We passed an Eskimo village but it was devoid of any sign of life. There was a big heap of garbage the Eskimos move the village from the garbage when it piles up, whereas we move the garbage. Some Innuk had already gone north to follow the snow as they must do when the days grew warmer. The Indians on the other hand would go south to hunt. Indians wore skins which they bartered with the Hudson Bay Company for western clothes.

As we passed the Hudson Bay Depot Father stopped and said,

"We have to get something for the mother and child."

"Like what?" I said. "Should I bring something?" I asked.

"Well would you like be the God Father?" he said.

"Me! Well glory be to God. That's impossible. How am I supposed to keep in touch with an Indian family to be a godfather?"

"He will have your name, Patrick Joseph"

"Good grief, give him a good Italian name," I said feeling like a bigot with name pride.

"Name him 'Patricus' Father or for the rest of his life people will be asking him what part of Ireland he's from." We bought tobacco and food gifts then set off. Huughuaq, huughuaq- get a move on faster faster Father cried encouraging the team. The dogs scrambled and barked as they pulled us across the rough surface around the store while the sled went rocking from side to side. Father looked up at the sky and cracked a whip over the lead dog. The sound reverberated through the pack as we accelerated.

Confused, mixed feelings, I could not see what was in my power to change until we could stop and I had time to think. The sledge was now moving fast on a downhill trail. We could see smoke from the village. Father glanced again at the sky. I was aware that we could not stay long as there was no way I could see to unhitch the dogs and tie them to poles. I realised that the child needed a Godfather and I had to be it. I didn't mind really but I felt the way father went about it that I had been had. I remember the squaw covering her breast modestly as she suckled her baby and felt me staring rudely. I thought she was a beautiful woman. Six months without even talking to an intelligent woman was a long time for any man!

We stood for the baptism. I held a container while the priest did the baptism ceremony which was the fruit of work and teaching. We ate a little, sometimes laughed. I recall the shy look on the squaw's face as she picked dried soft moss, which was hanging to dry on a cord and used it to change the baby no sooner had we got into the tent but it needed attention. The height of the Indian, who was taller than Father, himself over six feet tall, was impressive.

My bashfulness I felt was making everybody shy and ill at ease. I could not figure if this was a beginning of something or if it would end when we got outside the camp. What was the point of being a Godfather if one could not see the child again? Before getting on the sledge I put a twenty dollar bill in the baby's tiny hand and said farewell. With the Hudson Bay prices twenty dollars was equal to five in the south.

I wondered how the priest overcame loneliness while spending years here. I never saw or heard of the Indian boy again. Within the week the Indian villagers headed south and soon after I would be heading south to Montreal.

*It has been to common an error in regarding the the climate of the arctic regions, to take into consideration the lines of latitude only; and on the principle of considering the equator and the poles as the greatest heat and the greatest cold, to infer that in advancing northward the temperature will in all cases be found to correspond with the latitude. Nowhere, however are the inferences drawn from such views more erroneous than in the arctic regions, where the temperature depends in a great measure on the currents and drift-ice, the influence of which is remarkable..

Winter island in lat66 30N.,is consequently the pole of cold of the northern hemisphere during the summer; while Yakutsk, in Siberia ,may be taken as the winter pole. Winter Island is likewise the phytological north pole-namely, that point which possess the smallest number of genera and species of plants, and whence the number increases in every direction.

Quote. Chamber's Repository.

CHAPTER TEN

California

August 1961

As I did on most Sunday afternoons in Montreal, I donned my parka, overshoes, muffler and cowl and manoeuvred the icy pavement, in thirty to forty degrees below zero and went to the store to buy the paper. Inside the cosy store while browsing the forecast, I noticed that in Los Angeles the weather was 70 degrees. "How could there be a difference of 40 below to 70 above I asked myself, since it is winter in both places?" I decided to leave the hospitable people of Quebec provence and go to Los Angeles. at least for a time. I had a good livelihood in Quebec but the heavy weather after five years 'pointed the compass' to sunny California. I told myself I could always come back to Quebec, but faltered at the thought reflecting that I said the same thing leaving Ireland.

The confinement of the air force base for two years was ideal for study and allowed me to get a diploma in Cost Accounting; however, when in California, I could not see myself sitting at a desk for the rest of my life and decided after three years to return to my original trade, Communications. I went to San Mateo College for two years and got a Federal Communications licence a week after becoming a citizen.

On the first day so many of students enrolled that many had to stand in the rear of the classroom. The class opened with a word of caution from the teacher.

"Be advised! Eighty two percent of you will probably quit the class before the year is out or fail to get a license, if you don't think you can cut the mustard, now is the time to leave". At that cheerful introduction what seemed like half of the class walked out, leaving a few seats vacant. I gathered strength, having left Aer Lingus after two years as a grade B radio mechanic at Dublin airport; otherwise I would probably have walked. One thing I had in common with father was difficulty with maths.

But why go to sea to face deprivation, turbulence and what my mother in a 'mood' classed as depravity (!) and become a figure for people to conjure with. Actually it made a lot of sense and here's one good reason.

San Francisco is noted for troubles over the years with unions. Movies have been made and books written about the struggle between workers and companies. It is probably the strongest Union City in the world. The union I would join, the 'Marine Engineers Beneficial Association' (ROU), had the 'bull by the horns' when it came to union contracts... In the seventies there were over four thousand American merchant ships in the nineties there were around four hundred. The goose that laid the golden egg had been devastated from paying big compensation to crews. Companies began to use 'Foreign Flags' which meant paying Liberians and Panamanians a fraction of our wages for their labour.

As a Master Radio Electronics Officer in the U.S. Merchant Marine in 1972 I earned $12,000.00 a month, plus 'three hots and a cot', a good pension, six months annual vacation and I received fifteen thousand dollars vacation money every year to boot! It wasn't movie money, but where, on land, could I earn as much. Today Radio Officers are redundant because of the development in communications which was to a great extent made possible by the advances in industry to get in the race to the moon. In fact, even the captain's job I understand has for the most part been replaced by the Chief Engineer.

In the seventies we had Radio Officers, Radio Electronic Officers and Master Radio Electronic Officers. The latter spent two months a year in college and were competent to service every bit of electronic equipment on the ship including computers. I spent two months a year in college for three years before getting my Diploma. As an MREO, my pay with overtime, exceeded the captain's (who was on a fixed salary), such was the strength of the Radio Officer's Union. We were employed by various companies while the Union kept control of our pensions and medical care and sent us to varying slots to work for shipping companies.

At my first interview for an assignment in the Union Hall, a strange thing happened. The clerk picked up the phone and said

"My God! This is incredible." He turned to me and said,

"I'm terribly sorry, I have to leave right away. Captain Brown refuses to disembark!"

"Why is that?" I rejoined.

"He's afraid to put his foot on land! I have to meet a psychologist at the ship to solve his problem, so I must leave right away. Can you come back this afternoon at let's say two o'clock?"

"Of course, see you then"

That captain, like an animal, had subconsciously marked his territory and he just couldn't leave it! I became a bit apprehensive at the thought of a man in charge of a ship going out of control in this way. After some years at sea, I found it less difficult to understand. The most traumatic emotion after death and divorce is losing the home. The ship is the home and every inch of it is attended to with great care.

'Sail Ho!' I was a landsman beginning work on a ship. Except for a trip from Dublin to Holyhead I had never been on a ship. Our ship was called the Santa Magdalena, a combination cargo and cruise ship. I changed from casual dress to a white uniform with one chevron shining in the sun. I had my seaman's papers but no experience of the job or life at sea. The big question was having or acquiring the necessary sea legs.

As we left the harbour we went through the constant strange and dangerous turbulence from the waters leaving the estuary the same on return which is called the 'potato patch'.

I felt listless. The ship was pitched about in a sudden utter confusion for about twenty minutes in what looked like a sea of huge balloons. The crew went about their business paying no heed to things moving about on deck. They had their sea legs, left foot forward while the ship rolled in the other direction. It was all in a days work. I did not know how long it was going to last, (and grew listless) and the symptoms of seasickness were not helped when I began to worry about the effect it would have on my work, on this, the first day onboard.

We finally got out of the potato patch and beyond the bar. The ship went into a nice steady roll outside the 'gate' and headed south. It was a beautiful day of a pinkish Californian sun and stillness. It wasn't until I went into the cabin where, while checking equipment, the smell of aged puke got to me, and that triggered a heave over the side. I have never been on any ship that didn't have a slight odour of puke no matter how well the ship was attended.

I felt a nervous pitiable sight after 'the patch' for the first day but my spirits came back after a sound sleep. I arose to a calm sea as we were now well under way, sailing down the bay, for a long voyage through Panama around Colombia, Argentina and on to the Straits of Magellan, stopping at Santos and Rio. On the return voyage we stopped at Valparaiso Chile returning to San Francisco and then continue on up to Alaska. It took awhile before I developed the wide step and rolling gait of the real 'salt'.

I basked in the sun as the ship moved slowly through the Panama Canal and enjoyed every moment of it as we were headed for Cartagena. We had three Radio Officers on board and. were allowed to mingle with the passengers, who had paid the huge sum of eighteen thousand dollars each for the voyage.

I walked a quarter of a mile of deck, every day after watch weather permitting, with changing scenes and surprises. Accompanying us for long periods were friendly killer sharks, in my mind the most graceful and beautiful fish in the sea. Playful dolphins and whales we often saw. Only once did I see an albatross which often is spoken of a beautiful bird thought to bring bad luck. The sea was a dull grey which may have accounted for it appearing like a bird made from different skeletons.

My next voyage on a ship was to be my worst ever. It was on a huge container ship which turned out to be a disaster.

CHAPTER ELEVEN

Resentment sunk our ship

Resentment has killed relationships, caused many wars between our ancestors. Princes fought princes for little reason, a tiff or some annoyance no matter how petty, such as the resentment about the *Bo Cuilin . It has brought down many corporations. Companies, instead of focusing on improvements to cope with competition, have instead wasted time and money on legalities trying to hurt one another. Resentment can also sink a ship. If the relationship on the bridge; between the all-powerful captain and the mate become tested during a navigational decision; as it did on our ship the SS American trader, when 'Davy Jones' was a winner. Rages festered to the point that in high seas some wished the ship would sink.

Friday the thirteenth of February was the day arranged upon for the sailing of SS Sherwood, on a voyage from San Francisco across the Pacific to the island of Guam. Sailors are known to be a superstitious lot. In the rules for sailing the high sea there is a notification that no ship shall sail on Friday the thirteenth. This rule was obeyed in the old sailing days. Once there was a storm that sunk every ship in the Atlantic Ocean in the eighteen hundreds. Most ships which foundered had left on Friday the thirteenth.

As she was to get under way before midday, I boarded the night before. It was a comfortable ship. I had a large state cabin complete with built in stereo, TV and refrigerator. I changed from my street clothes to my light loose fitting khaki uniform, made my pre - sailing tests and then had a light meal in the galley before turning in. I was conscious of the fact that I would have four hours sleep and four hours watch for the next six months or so, which has always been the most difficult part of a sailor's lot, especially on the sailing ships of the past. We must adjust to the changing time zones and the body's 'clocks' are forever changing trying to get accustomed to this. Getting sufficient sleep is the seaman's preoccupation and constipation has always been the seaman's curse. I skipped dairy foods and have been told that I am 'overly fond' of the bed on land.

The Radio Officer has a difficult watch. The news comes at perhaps four in the morning by the Morse code, at twenty, sometimes twenty-five words a minute and one should be able to type at forty-five w.p.m. to work comfortably. He never knows when the captain will call on him to send or receive messages and in bad weather he has to send position reports (AMVER) hourly.

We left San Francisco harbour, facing heavy weather. The 'potato patch' was as rough as it could be. After the nausea of the 'patch' the ship slowed down and we let the pilot off. It is strange that at that time, far from the land, as the ship comes to a stop and the pilot climbs down the Jacob's ladder there comes a momentary feeling of loneliness and foreboding when sailors know they have months of hard work ahead and they will be occupied and little is in their power to change. Once across the bar, having let off the pilot, we headed across the Pacific. Everybody on the ship was busy at this time and we looked forward to the first watch to be over to get some sleep before facing heavy seas.

Starting a long voyage one is greatly concerned to work comfortably with shipmates, otherwise it could be most unpleasant. The smallest trifles cause quarrels that might otherwise be laughed off. Things can linger on for the length of a voyage, often coming to a boil on the waterfront usually in a bar where I have seen the saddest scenes of fist fighting among American Navy Officers

On this, my worst voyage, and I would say the same for the rest of the crew, there was little laughter or getting along right from embarking on the ship. In fact our voyage was crowded with resentful incidents that mushroomed into a bitter stupor between the Captain, the First Mate and the Company. The Captain with a pursed mouth full of anger and resentment and mute most of the time, was almost helpless on the bridge whenever the Mate was around. Life on a ship is difficult at the best of times and strange to those who have not gone to sea for long periods.

There was no need to carry a wallet or worry about food or bills while at sea. I don't think many landlubbers can really understand the effect a sea going life without daily money transaction can have on a man. We have a saying, 'spending money like a sailor six months at sea'. The purpose and function of money becomes so unclear that mariners are easily duped and suffer 'rip offs' at the waterfront and elsewhere.

The seaman's life is a peculiar occupation because he is acting in a world stage and with a narrow intricate interplay of personality in the confined space of a ship. If things are going well it is a great life, but when things go wrong you are trapped in a bizarre world with no way or place to walk.

The most important relationship is between the Captain, the Mate and the Chief Engineer. If the Captain finds fault with the Mate for mishandling the crew or for some other reason and starts cribbing with the mate or the chief engineer, then the crew and everybody suffers, becoming discontented as a result. Every eye bat is noticed on a ship. To return to the SS American trader, I must mention that before we left we were anchored three miles off the coast of San Francisco, delayed because of some problem with an engine part. We enjoyed a beautiful mild morning with a red pinkish sun, while breakfasting in the galley. The sea was calm and was speckled over with white sailing, fishing and pleasure boats in the distance. I ate cod fish, sauté potatoes, brown bread and coffee, while relaxing with reading the World Tribune. Two deck officers and the Chief Engineer bid good morning and took a place at the table. As I was finishing breakfast they asked for the Captain's whereabouts, as the Captain's seat was vacant, as it was to remain for the whole voyage. Sailors are a notably suspicious lot. The empty chair seemed a 'bad omen'. I thought how little we know what would happen to us any minute of our lives and to cheer myself up, I told myself that when matters look bad, very often the best is in store for us, but it was not to be.

With a bad weather forecast chart, I headed for my first encounter with the Captain. As I made my way to the bridge, all the crew were active, some busy painting, others getting the stores, boats were plying around us. I went to the skipper's quarters. The six foot two old man was standing at the door in a heavy woollen tartan robe with a face as long as the leg of his pyjamas.

"Are you ok, Captain?" I enquired, thinking that he might either complain or explain or send me to hell. He tightened the cord on his robe and said in a soft deliberate voice

"I need my medicine".. Real medicine I wondered. God! Don't tell me, he's in need of a bottle, a crutch; what was going on? He looked livid. He took the weather report, glanced at it and pushed it aside as if he couldn't handle any more bad news. I made copies for the First Mate and the boson; so the crew could prepare for foul weather with possibly forty feet waves. After climbing a few decks, I returned to the Captain's room; when in walked a company officer, with a mate who had just got his license and was going to ride along for the '*experience*' which was strange and hard to imagine.. He handed the captain the sailing instructions in a briefcase. The Captain glanced through them, turned to the representative and said "I want this Mate off the ship immediately" He paused and said.

"Where's Mitchell?" (regular company representative), he asked the man named Kelly.

Shaking like a leaf, the Captain almost tore the bag asunder while hopefully searching for his 'medicines'. He found diabetic medicine, then said

"Where's *the* medicine, what the fuck is going on here? 'Sparks' get me Mitchell on the blower."

"It's after office hours Skipper, he's not at the office". I replied hoping he might cool off before calling.

"Well get him at home, or wherever the hell he is, damn it Sparks!"

It was uppermost in our minds what 'medicine' the captain was alluding to, but none of us ventured to advert to what it was, because of his vacillating temper. Mitchell's wife answered the phone.

"Mrs Mitchell this is the Radio Officer on the American Trader, the Captain would like to have a word with Mr. Mitchell"

"Well he's having his dinner can it wait awhile?"

"I'm sorry, but it is urgent" The Captain, sweating, hands trembling grabbed the phone.

"I need to talk to John right now. Margaret can you get him to the phone, where is he?"

"Mitchell! What happened to my fucking medicine and the regular Mate? What's the idea of sending this fucker (mate) on board without my permission over?"

"Sorry! Sean, I couldn't get to the pilot with the 'stuff' anyway you'd better ask Jeff, and calm down, because in case you've forgotten by the way, he *owns* the company. It was Jeff's idea to let the mate ride without pay for the experience".

"I'm sending this fucker off the ship now; he cannot do that without signing papers?"

It's not supposed to be that way for sure" said Mitchell.

"What the fuck does he think he's doing? He can't do that!"

"As I said Captain, he owns the fucking company, you tell him."

I had illusions before as to what was happening, I had none now, it was clear the Skipper had the 'hibbee jeebees'. We were getting the 'willies' at the thought of spending three months on board with this carry on. He was being held in check by the owner and was cornered without his booze.

I guessed from the conversation that the new mate had more than one reason to be onboard. A Captain seldom interferes with a Mate doing his work. If he does, the forebodings can be grim for the Mate. To tell the Mate the Captain wanted him off the ship before leaving the dock was cruel.

Standing in a daze, the Captain was still in his pyjamas, offset by us in uniform. We entered his quarters to 'sign on'. When finished, he banged his desk with his fist feeling let down by a man he had sailed with for twenty years, Mitchell, (a retired captain himself) who was now an executive and his onshore boss.. The usual meetings of mind before a voyage, which makes us comfortable, was instead making us a little pissed even before leaving the harbour. I had never seen that happen before. The old man became an irritant to the crew and it was a blessing we had a good Boatswain whose calmness kept the crew happy and busy. The captain went to the press, poured the last two fingers of a 'Murphy's whiskey', tossed the bottle through the porthole and turned the Hi Fi. down. It played O'Donnell Abu continuously; ah feck, one of our own like this. He kept his distance from me. I felt it was because he knew he was hurting us both in our Irish pride by his behaviour. I reached for the 'hand piece', signed off and was relieved to see him pick up the bad weather report. It was a sad state of affairs. Soon into the voyage, he had the second mate check to make sure none of the crew had liquor and if they had, he must confiscate it. As we were under way, grey streaks ran along the western horizon with some clouds darkening the face of the sea. Heading far from the land we saw the last of the mountains that surround the lovely city of San Francisco. The snowy buzzing televisions were turned off, the radios turned on. We welcomed work and kept busy to alleviate the thoughts of deprivation and remind ourselves of the compensation at the end of the voyage. For a couple of weeks we had a long spell of good weather with quiet seas and some squalls. Better than the forecast. Then there came southerly gales, storms and torrential rain continuing until we were midway. As the third mate was on his way to give the captain the disappointing news that the ship was 'dry', he was troubled with the thought as to why an A.B. should have a large bottle of bleach in his quarters and feared that further down the log he might discover that it contained whiskey. If he returned below deck he would probably find the bottle missing and if he found it, it might have worse consequences for the Captain he thought. He decided to leave it.

Ugh! Ugh! Was there anything worse than a voyage through a low of 650 with forty to fifty feet waves! On one watch, I reported fifty-five feet high waves to the coast guard. Captains are confined to their quarters most of the day, they enjoy time spent on the bridge, while working and for companionship. The days went by, then the weeks. It seemed that our 'old man' might be seen at the bridge, perhaps three or four times a week up and down. He had diabetes and his feet seemed swollen. His meals were brought to his cabin. He never ate in the dining room..

If a captain has a close friend (besides his dignity), it is usually the RO or the Medic. He goes ashore with either one because they do not 'work' with the crew I suppose. In the past they were known as 'sleeping crew'. I saw our captain for daily communication of ship business and that was it. He was mostly out of humour and I feared for his health.

I sent a message reporting fifty-foot waves as mentioned and the breakage of six heavy steel containers on the bow. The front of each had been hit so hard by the waves they opened to the wind and the contents vanished. At times in heavy weather like this, conversation was usually kept level, with course jokes or waterfront talk, even bouts of song to lift the courage when the waves were really threatening. As the crew became aware that the Mate and Captain were not talking to each other, life aboard grew tedious.. By the day the Mate kept the men busy with overtime work

A Captain's cardinal rule on any ship is 'never to criticise the Mate in front of any of the crew, if he does, it's a sign he wants the mate off the ship'. If this happens things become lax and the crew demoralized. It would have been better if they had been at swords point rather than this non-seaman like carry-on. Sometimes some of the crew seemed to be sleepwalking. The mate, shunned and resented, probably learned nothing from the captain. In fact, in the middle of heavy weather, at times the mate looked as if he wished the ship would sink and end it all.

One night after a rough watch I had just fallen asleep and was at about 'periscope depth' at four o'clock, when I heard a loud bang on my cabin door. I opened it to behold the mate waving a pink form, an 'Amber reading', saying.

"Hay Sparkeee, what doo I doo wid….diss….fuukinn….thiiiing?"

"Wod you wand matee, Oowhaat….Fookinnn….thing," I mimicked.

He had a glimmer of a smile, while I tried my hardest not to burst out laughing tired as I was, realising how his depression made him drawl, as if he was drunk and that, believe me, is one of the effects of heavy seas - a form of intoxication.

It was a glorious warm evening, though extremely humid and hot.

The following day when we cheerfully saw land at Guam, we received a message by radio that there was no bar pilot available for twenty four hours. The Captain decided to bring the ship into the harbour himself. He stood forward and for the first time in uniform, on the bridge. An AB behind him at the wheel, the Mate was out on the port wing and the third mate was reading maps with an electric light with a curtain around him oblivious to everything. I was standing outside the navigation room at the rear. The captain had been in and out of the harbour for twenty years. He probably felt he needed to do the company a favour after his run in with Mitchell "Captain, we have to change course we are too near the pier," the mate intimated from the outer wing. The captain didn't respond. I was too far to the rear of the bridge to know for sure. Minutes went by then the mate entreated once more.

"Captain, we may hit the pier, can we change course?". I don't believe this I said out loud. I walked forward beside the old man who stood as if frozen. We had two or three minutes to adjust the course. Stepping back to the chart room, I jerked back the curtain and said to the third mate who was standing and looking into space. "Listen you had better come out mate, we're in trouble, we might crash the dock, the captain isn't with it". He gave me a stare, as if to say 'what can a 'third' do between the chief mate and captain without getting his head cut off'. He said in a low, inward looking voice

"I know, I can hear" and slowly closed the curtain. Feeling useless, I walked over towards the wheel, looked over the bow and saw clearly that it was too late for anyone to do something; we were going to climb the rocks.

We stood on the bridge aghast as the Chief Mate warned the captain, three times minutes apart, that if we held the course, we would hit the rocks, and hit the rocks we did. The hull was torn with a steep gash of about five metres..

Cupping his hands around his mouth, the Mate gave a roar to the captain. As a horrible sounding jarring noise vibrated throughout the ship we came slowly to a stop, perched upon the rocks at the entrance to Guam harbour. It was strange that I was not a bit angry. I had a lump in my throat and a sinking guilty feeling that no one befriended the captain and perhaps myself in particular. I felt as if my soul was damaged somehow and wondered what was wrong with our nature to cause such loneliness among us. It is said that a pack of wolves has one soul which seems a better nature than this. We were relieved the day after to learn that the ship's torn side could be filled with concrete and she could then be towed to a dry dock for repair. This was done the next day.

The S.S. American Trader ran aground entering the port of Guam, an island infested with a type of snake that ate everything. Little notice was taken of our big container ship as it left their island in tow to the dry dock for repairs except for a note in the newspapers.

Resentment reminds me of blood pressure, in the sense that they are both 'silent killers'; one of the body the other of the soul. Large companies were driven out of business, because, instead of acting to find a way to beat the attack of a competitor, resentment paralysed directors and misdirected their energies. They could not get their minds 'on the ball' and do things constructively.

When we got into Guam the custom of sailors buying full rounds, the hearty cheer of brotherhood and sea stories were not to be. I think we just could not get off the ship mentally, nor remove the pain and the stupidity of the whole affair. We now had to fly back to San Francisco to the shipping hall to find a slot for another ship. One gets accustomed to a ship like a home and the crew know each other. It so happened that the SS. American Trader was in dry dock for only six weeks before being seaworthy and most of the crew made it back to that ship.

We fanned out more as 'loners' than a happy crew to expensive hotel bars, disgusted with everything. Our captain, the prime minister of the ship, the man with supreme power, who disciplined each one of us, had given in to prideful feelings or whatever caused our ship to go under, not all the way, luckily, but under the wash.

It was the absence of a bar pilot, who for some reason could not arrive onboard that had made the captain decide to steer the ship into the harbour. He had seen the pilot do it many times and if he and the mate had been more focused, it would have gone O.K. in my opinion. In trying to save the company money by not parking outside the harbour for twenty-four hours he almost totally lost the ship. If the captain and the mate had their heads together they probably would not have gone in and would have waited for the following day, when the pilot might have arrived. None the less, I believe that if there were a meeting of the minds between the mate and the captain, the ship would not have hit the rocks.

The crew felt let down badly. It was the first time I had seen such a bad disposition of a crew from the beginning of a voyage to the end. Prime ministers, kings and princes cause wars in the same bad spirit. 'Wars are pleasant to leaders', as the Romans say. "Foolish youth instead of shooting their officers, go to war to have a pistol at the back of their heads". G. B. Shaw. Voltaire remarked "murder is not murder if done in a uniform"

The captain who I thought would be jailed during the investigation of the incident, got away I heard with only two years suspension of his seaman's papers. I wish him and the mate better joss! The captain had the best and most trustworthy record over many years but was now a sick man.

I was tired of people and deprivation. Minor trifles can produce quarrels on shipboard but what we had experienced was devastating. I think most of the crew like myself felt underrated and isolated because on a ship more than on land people live in one another's shelter. There are some who when off the ship live in cheap hotels in frightening solitude that saps the mind, pushed apart into a lonely world.

Instead of flying to the States with the crew; sick of the sea, I went from Guam to Singapore and lived it up for a week in the Sofital Hotel, There was a copy of the bible on one side table and the Koran on the other. Good for a mixed marriage! I thought because there is so much written in those books, encouraging men to live in peace. Life became more of a mystery with the day.

I decided to stay in Singapore for a few months and moved into a cheaper hotel. I came 'out of the writer's closet' and began the solitary business of writing, as an escape from the experience on the ship, but I did not intend to stop sailing. The need to keep writing became a part of me and as I wrote of my childhood, involuntary memories came flooding in. My writing time seemed to follow my watches on the ship. Yes! the good ship the S.S. American trader, four hours in the morning, another four hours in the evening until I produced this semi-memoir.

*A prize bull that was fought over by Irish royalty.

CHAPTER TWELVE

Aim high Alongapo

T wo years after the Guam disaster, I was on the S.S. Sherwood sailing into this beautiful tropical bay with the ever green on its surrounding mountains forming a lush canopy, men-of-war boats plying unceasingly to and fro across the tranquil water of the bay. Huge warships and other killing machines slowly crossed each other's courses. There were great warring vessels with many pennants, giving a fiesta effect. Launches buzzed past the small fishing boats which were everywhere and seemed oblivious to their surrounding. Their minds were on fish!

One Aircraft Carrier docked cathedral like, dwarfed the buildings alongside. My ship, a refuelling navy ship, SS Windemere,188500 DWT, full of oil, had come through a storm in the Baring Straits during which the assault of the waves was such that this vessel, invincible as it was, made us feel at times as if we were on a barge.. Lifts were knocked out of commission which meant walking up flights of deck to the Galley. The steel hull had many scars, where paint had been removed and the bare steel glistened in the sun. Some areas had already rusted.

I was in a cheerful expectant mood as I climbed down the Jacob's ladder to the fast launch, which would take us to a bus and on to a transit point to leave the huge American base of Subic. A few of the crew had already had a drink on the ship (which was illegal) and were shaking to and fro as the long twenty meter ladder swayed dangerously. This happens if the rhythmic movement of the hands to grip the rope isn't done before moving the feet. All eyes were upon one shipman, as we held our breath while he manoeuvred down with one arm in a sling and had insisted on coming to see the town... We sped by launch to the passport office where our passports were checked and we passed through the grill gate which led directly to a bridge into the town of Alongapo.

It was the dry season. People held tissues to their noses and held their breath because the river, (Bgnicgin I believe) reeking with human faeces (which in my mind stinks worst in the animal kingdom), moved slowly like Volcanic lava.

On the bridge stood a group of about fifteen young navy officers, dressed in glowing white uniforms with brass shining in the sun while a coin was thrown into the river, a boy dived in, retrieved it to a loud cheer and then officers continued throwing coins into the filthy water. Young boys with sickly bony faces dived in to retrieve the coins, which may have been the only means they had of buying a bowl of rice. They would surface at last; shake themselves like fish in a net, covered in filth and faeces, then hold up the retrieved coins triumphantly!

"Strike one" roared eight or ten navy officers standing on the bridge which excited a general roar of laughter, cheers and applause. I stood flabbergasted on the bridge. My blood began to boil in the ninety degree heat. The sweat rolled down my forehead in helpless dismay as I stood dumfounded on the bridge.

"Jesus help me" I said to myself.

"Let's get to hell out of here I said to a shipmate while all I could do was grumble at the cheering 'Gentlemen officers'.

I was alone, no one cared. Overcome by it all, I did a stupid thing. I waved at a crowd of elderly Filipinos standing on the bank and pointed to children dressed in school uniforms, watching this ugly humiliating performance and motioned to them, arms out, to do something to stop this mocking bizarre performance.

I found myself in the position of advancing on what had become my adversary, American navy men. The Filipino men bowed their heads nodding in disgust and frustration. An officer seeing my motivation looked at me in a way that I felt he had tattooed the mark of Cain on my forehead for betrayal and that he wished to throw me into the river , For a minute, I wished I could have thrown the whole lot of them in the river.

My day, the day I had been looking forward to for months on rough high seas, suddenly became very burdensome after only one hour on Filipino soil. My expectation for a good R & R vanished because these men suddenly were no longer brothers of the sea in fact, standing at that horrible scene on the bridge, there were moments when I hated the lot of them, every son of Uncle Sam for their affront to the human dignity of these simple people.

"No one else seems to give a damn, why should I?" I persuaded myself.

I hastily walked a hundred yards beyond the bridge where a gentle breeze cooled me and tenderly carried the odour of the river towards the mountains. The streets were crowded. I fully realized that liquor would contribute to my problems yet I couldn't resist that initial shockwave of confidence it gave me I ordered two San Miguel beers, at twenty five cents a bottle. After deprivation and heavy seas, one is entitled to a drink, a few 'sea stories' and fraternal fellowship but this day there was no rainbow of hope for that.

The lovely, gaudy colours of the Jeepneys (small buses) were a colourful break in the drab scene of the waterfront. They were bumper to bumper; all spewing out leaded exhaust fumes, as they avoided the potholes. While riding across the potholes, the thumb would punch the baby's thumb through or against its palate if it was sucking it.

A boy sat in the doorway, a boy with a tin cup (I ignored him) and beside him sat a dog whose ribs were showing through its hide, where the hair had fallen off in large areas and with bleeding patches across its back from the blistering heat of the sun. He whined to a rage as he tried to reach the sores on its back with its tongue. I offered the dog a candy while cautioned by the waiter to leave him alone and not to pet him, because he "goes for the Huevos". Dogs were overly friendly for the hope of a scrap of food. Most were starving and running wild.

Turning back, as I left I saw the boy just miss a kick to the dog, as the animal sensed what to expect and cleverly ducked. As I walked the dusty streets of the town, here and there stepping over a drain, avoiding an air conditioner projecting on to the pavement and dripping moisture as if removing the sweat of those inside, it appeared as if every woman on the street was 'available'. The 'smell' of sex was everywhere. A lot of men were in the business of sex. The chatter of the day was sex and how to push it and get the best return from the six thousand prostitutes that served mostly the American seamen and a sprinkling of visitors.

The town seemed lacking of a decent community spirit, or even a good family life for that matter, because there wasn't the freedom to bring up children without exposing them to the grotesque.

When one looks at the behaviour of the officers on the bridge and life in Alongapo and the price we Americans gave to have what *our idea of civilisation should be* most cruelly planted on the Vietnamese, who are just a short distance across the water from here, it makes one wonder if we are verged on madness and evil in the world we live in, and in the way we have contributed to it.

I have an imperfect recollection of events in a bar, the night of the scene on the bridge in Alongapo (Subic). I know the drink worked strong that night and destroyed my sensibility as I wished it to. I believe I shed tears beside the dancing girls and, with a hiccup, told them I wished I were way back home in Ireland which made them laugh. For days I was angered at the thought of the boys that could easily have perished in that filth. My thoughts

The Movement behind the Savings Certificate

REALISE how great—how inspired—the work of the Savings Movement is.

To-day there are 31,109 Savings Associations, and 150,000 workers in the Movement—*voluntary and unpaid.*

They would not go on devoting to it their time and energies in this unselfish way, if it were not remarkably worthy.

Why do they do it? Because each in his own way perceives, and wishes everyone to perceive, that the more all of us can rightly save, the greater, in a little while, will be not only our wealth, but our prosperity and contentment—both individually and nationally. So, having faith, they work steadily on.

It remains only for you to do your part—to buy Savings Certificates, *and to save to buy more,* just as steadily.

Thus you can make yourself, your family and your country the better off.

Will you?

Savings CERTIFICATES

Obtainable through a Savings Association, or from any Bank, Money Order Post Office or Official Agent. Or you can buy them by instalments by asking at any Post Office for 6d. Savings Stamps and a card (free) on which to stick them.

15/6	—	£1 : 0 : 0	—	£1 : 6 : 0
To-day		In five years		In ten years

The Swastika was a lucky sign the world over before the war.

Which ?

A WORD TO PARENTS

' Extravagance rots character ; train youth away
rom it. The habit of saving money stiffens the
vill and brightens the energies.''—Theodore
Roosevelt.

Look to the future of your children. A great
eal depends on you. It is not too early to begin
ow to put aside as much as you can each week
r month to help your children's start in life. You
o not want them to drift into a '' blind alley ''
ccupation that leads no where. Their future may
epend on having a sum of money at hand when
ey leave school to help in their further training
or a profession or calling.

Not only should you yourself save, but you
ould encourage the children in habits of thrift,
orethought, and discipline.

See that your children are members of the
SCHOOL SAVINGS ASSOCIATION,
hich provides a practical thrift lesson. Even a
nny can be saved through an Association.

How small sums grow in 5 years : —

6d. a week becomes	£7	1	6.
1/-	,,	,,	£14	4	6
2/-	,,	,,	£28	11	6
2/6	,,	,,	£36	2	5
3/-	,,	,,	£43	7	3
4/-	,,	,,	£57	17	2
5/-	,,	,,	£72	7	1
7/-	,,	,,	£101	6	10

Spend wisely and make a habit of regularly buying.

urchase price 15/-   Value in 5 years £1.

Advantages include : State Security, 5¼ per cent.
mpound Interest, Easy Repayment, and Freedom
m Income Tax.

On sale at all Banks and Money Order Post
fices.

Write for full particulars (no stamp required) to the
CENTRAL SAVINGS COMMITTEE,
65 Dawson Street,
H.Co 18.   DUBLIN.

cLub nA múinceóiní náisiunca—MEMBERS OF FIRST COMMITTEE, 192:

(Some members were unavoidably absent when the group was being taken.)

ack Row—F. J. O'Doherty (hon treas) W. Hare, J. A. Cosgrave, J. Herlihy, T. J. Gillespie, I arolan. Third Row—M. Fitzpatrick, T. Brady, Miss A. Nolan, P. Brookes, Miss B. Holey, i 1. Murphy, P. J. Quinn, E. Maguire. Second Row—Miss A. Kennedy, T. D. O'Brien (hon. : ; C. Finegan (Pres.), Miss M. J. Proctor (V.Pres.), P. Cummins (V.Pres.), Miss L. Batty, T. Ha Front Row—Miss B. Clare, Miss A. Hilton

*Uncle Jim with the revolver mother many times hid in her cloths when
the Brits put the inevitable X on our door to be searched.
He died from pneumonia caused by living in ditches on the run.*

Caught on the hop with tears, I surprised the sisters with a camera

Well anchored with shoes a size too big and Eva's hand knit comfortable woollen socks, two of the many gifts received. When the great Marshal de Saxes was asked, after winning many battles of the Emporer. "What was the happiest day of your life?" He astounded his generals by replying "The day I made my first communion". The happiest day of most people's lives, used to be the day they made their first Communion and so it was with me.

Having told all my sins bravely.

Age four. Eva's hand knitted Jersey with buttons.

Father on the left.

Top left: Sister Eva Cris
Smith, friend and me after a
haircut.

Tattered and torn, the only
photo of Mother.
Mother 1916

1997

clung to the beautiful hills that surrounded Alongapo and the lush forests with the tall palm trees and beautiful tropical sunsets and the minute detail of what happened on the bridge. Most of all, the half-stifled cries of the young schoolgirls in their gay blue uniforms at the horror seeing the boys covered in filth from the river.

The following day the sun had risen about an hour, the fatigue of the previous day had impressed me but I was determined to take a hurried breakfast early in the morning and go the Post Office long before the heat of the day. The town was quiet,, dogs slept fitfully, a few nightclubs still had small twinkling lights on. Outside a bank there were three guards standing to attention with shotguns and pistols at the ready and three more inside. As I entered the P.O., I met a man who bespoke me in my own Dublin dialect. He was to become a close friend. His name was Fr. Shea Cullen. When we came outside I invited him to a coffee across the street. After we chatted awhile, I told him about a strange experience which I had a month previously, in a bar.

I walked into a nightclub on the outskirts of Alongapo. It was the early afternoon and three girls lay on the seats taking a nap as it was quiet. When they noticed my presence they sat up and right away a girl with a harelip was told to scoot in a rude manner. As she passed by, I looked into the saddest eyes I have ever seen while she melted into tears. It was difficult to look at the poor girl's melancholy face as she ran to the rear. Someone I screamed with insults at the girl in Galog. "I just want a beer, tell her to come back and enjoy her rest,"

I was so moved that the next day (aware of the power of the almighty dollar here) I enquired at a clinic about the cost of an operation for her, but I cannot remember the details as I had a drink or two. However I do remember a surgeon telling me that there were no facilities for such an operation in the city and I would have to send her to Manila. If a baby is in the womb and is sucking its thumb as the mother is bounced, it can cause harelip and damage the pallet. One of Father Shea Cullen's projects (a saintly man who comes into the story later) was addressing this problem and helping people. In a population of fifteen million, forty per cent of the population of the Philippines was under the age of sixteen and the average income in 1984 was $30 a month. One and a half million were blind from a vitamin deficiency. Alongapo is the first town in the world to produce a strain of gonorrhoea that was incurable.

After relating this to Father Cullen he told me that the health facilities were among the finest in the Orient and very reasonable at that! He explained what caused the harelip and why it was common in these parts. It is due to the rough riding and jumping in and out of Jeepneys when a

81

woman is pregnant... Those potholes were so big and the drivers went so fast that there was, and is a problem with harelip in the Philippines and other third world countries. He told me that he had founded an organisation to help those affected, when he first arrived in the Philippines in the way of education and aid. In alongapo the roads are full of potholes and there are some dreadful sights of hairlip. He was pleased to see my interest and invited me to visit him at PRADA. There and then I had an immediate affinity with the man. He sensed where the greatest need to relieve pain and suffering existed and had decided on his own initiative to find a solution. One thing for sure Fr. Cullen is not a 'golfing' priest and is actively engaged from eight in the morning till late in the evening, enthusiastic and zealous with Prada which is an organisation to help abused children.

The morning broke beautifully on Saturday as I walked through the long tracts of woods that moved onward from the sea to the big facility of PRADA Cullen's home for abused children. There it manufactures goods to help drug addicts, which are marketed around the world and back in Ireland, supermarkets like Superquinn, have delicious fruits from there. Cullen is a successful business man in his own right. I climbed some steps and after a brief introduction was ushered to a room where Cullen sat on a cushion, surrounded by a very well behaved group of children celebrating Mass in Tagalog. The children's responses were loud, clear and confident.

No doubt every child sitting there had there own story of abuse and misery. Only hours after they arrive, a transformation takes place and they have rekindled a child's spirit. The lovely, healthy lives they now enjoyed are simply 'manna from heaven'! This is another world, filled with joy, laughter and a love they have never experienced and for the first time they are fully clothed and fed decently. They recapture their innocence and trust in people. Some day Alongapo will build a monument in appreciation of what this man has done for the children in their country.

Cullen was responsible more that anyone else for getting the Subic base closed and, in my opinion, without his presence and work the base would still be open. This is not the only good he has done in the Philippines. Martin Sheen, the actor, and a group have put his name forward for the Nobel Peace prize for his work with abused children, In fact it was because of his work with children that the idea of closing the base became polarised and mushroomed in my opinion... A day to day scene in a hospital brought about more than anything else the evacuation of the U.S. Navy from the Philippines. The following is what happened (according to a newspaper).

One day a very distressed nun from the clinic in Alongapo came to visit Cullen. I understand she grew so emotional that when she went to talk to him she couldn't speak and just left in tears. He worried about this and the following day Cullen visited the clinic and insisted the nun tell him what was bothering her.

"Well Father, I will show you the problem," she ventured and took him to see two little girls, seven and nine years olds, who were being treated in the clinic and who had been raped by an American Naval Officer. Both were wounded, and were infected with gonorrhoea.

He was appalled and after a long silence decided to do the impossible and expose the suffering of the children and respond to the tyranny of the base and expose the American icons for what they really were. A committee of his facility sat upon the question and decided to have the naval officer prosecuted. Cullen requested an interview with the Admiral regarding a charge he intended making against the officer. Rumour went around the city that an American office might be charged with rape. But few believed it and most shrank from the thought in dread. Six thousand prostitutes had sleepless days no doubt. Mayor Gorden was infuriated. The American base with the thousands of military was the 'life blood' of the city and everybody kowtowed to the occupiers. The evening of the news a Filipino Monsignor and the Mayor appeared at PREDA (Cullen's residence) to discuss his radical views and to get an explanation. Cullen complained about the evils and not the base itself, none the less they advised against pursuing the charges...

Cullen dressed in jeans, a sport shirt and wearing a small wooden cross arrived at the Admiral's cabin on the aircraft carrier. Three officers dressed in spotless white uniforms with rows of decorations were standing, along with a man in civilian clothes, around the Admiral's desk which had a pile of papers upon it. Cullen looking at the admiral said "What are you going to do about the officer who raped these children? You can't just sweep it under the rug, it will be in the media" he pledged. To cut things short the officer was charged and things mushroomed and finally the Base was closed.

I returned to Alongapo in the late nineties. One became cheerfully aware of the mental hygiene in having got rid of the sordid sex business. If men are fishing all day they talk about fish or other healthy topics. If men are selling women and sex all day they talk about trading and enslaving people for profit. Morality is non existent. Man is the product of his environment. Once again there is beauty in the moon over Alongapo. The transformation in the people now that they were finding other occupations was palpable. The men are serious hard working people despite the poverty. There were no more 'barkers' soliciting nor more prostitutes than normal in any town. Women gave friendly looks rather than come hither signs. The smell of sex was replaced by the smell of fish, normal things and conversation was friendly, healthy and basic.

The hard coloured grey warships with all their pageants were as romantic as a motor generator. The absence of the huge killing machine, the J. F. Kennedy aircraft carrier (Big John), left a huge gap from when I previously saw it and the harbour seemed much larger. Other vessels had departed and except for one cruiser (which could have been a Filipino one) which circled past a buoy, life had reverted to a wholesome serenity. The small rainbow-coloured sailing boats were the very essence of romance. There were more fishing boats than ever, with their strange sails and double bottoms moved like swans. They had reposed most of the American scene now that there fleets had left and again it was uncompromisingly Filipino. Alongapo had risen. As I remembered, my stay in Alongapo, in 1984 the only Catholic country in the East was very pleasant despite everything I have related.

CHAPTER THIRTEEN

San Mateo

T he strong Spanish community in the San Francisco Bay Area's San Mateo church wore their sombreros and pointed shoes. The well groomed Italians and Irish wore their bawneen sweaters and tweed sports coats; The French women were immaculately dressed. Most of the congregation was predominant in business and religious affairs such as the Knights of Colombus. These were, for the most part, the congregation in this wealthy parish at the Sunday mass in the sixties when I arrived in San Mateo. The sound of birds was deafening. Beautiful woodpeckers punched holes into my english walnut trees. There must have been hundreds of species, but today because of the grey squirrel eating the bird eggs, one seldom sees a bird except for the odd blue jay or seagull expecting a storm and paying a goodwill visit to the area. The humming bird has survived the squirrels, probably because the eggs in their nests are out of reach, but because of their low flight pattern, cats have had a devastating effect on them. The grey squirrels are fat and plentiful in the parks, and almost look like vermin. Strange they kill the red squirrels also.

Over the years the community has been replaced by the colourful trimmed sleeved shirts and shorts of Asians mostly Chinese who now represent more than half of the population of the Bay area. They have enormous wealth and the Church is glad to have them. The young intellectual Catholic church of the sixties has become mostly a senior congregation while many have moved to Oregan .Churches were packed to the doors in those days. People elbowed to lean on a wall and one might only be able to barely hear the priest. In ten minutes the church was empty and the priest had a sudden lonely moment while finishing his task. After the service, outside in the gardens, smoke would rise from a barbecue for a Fiesta, a St. Pat's or a Fourteenth of July celebration. The priests at times would arrive play a violin or give us a song.

I have seen the changes over the past forty years and in the bay area of San .Francisco and having returned to Ireland have no doubt that in ten or fifteen years 'whites' could be in the minority in the republic of Ireland.

San Francisco, New Orleans, Montreal, and Buenos Aires are the most European cities in the Americas. The 1970 census in S.F counted 710,000.with 511,000 whites Asians were 59,000 Chinese, 25,000 Filipino and 12,000 Japanese, Today thirty years later white children are the minority in the bay area schools and even in the state of California. The Chinese are running the show.

Are we wrong to say that we wish to live in a society that is predominently Irish? There are now over a hundred thousand Chinese legal or illegal living in Ireland. These immigrants are not equally spread across the age groups but will be disproportionely concentrated in the thirties.and forties. The wealth and power will be in the Chinese community,(even with less numbers and when the second generation is not handy capped by not knowing English or Gaelig) as happened in the Philippines, (where in 2002 the people set about killing all Chinese) Indonesia, the San Francisco bay area, and other countries where they immigrated. All immigrants will outnumber their peers in five years perhaps but for sure in less than fifteen. The problem is that there is no suffering now to waken or warn us, but wait, as time passes, we will be outnumbered..

As I think of the suffering of five revolutions in two hundred years to recover Irish territory it makes me sad. It also disturbs me to feel that my judgement may be at variance with the majority of the young in Ireland who have not lived through the transformation that I have seen in the San Francisco bay area.

If these statements seem dogmatic so be it. I am not going to say 'I think' or 'for jaysus sake will ye listen' or 'di ye know what' or 'can ye just imagine' to be nice and bore people. These are not just wild predictions but a systematic study of facts with the experience of being in the many countries which have opened the gates to a flood of Chinese and are now run by them.

I am not a politician, but a mariner. This is about sorting out my thoughts on subjects that have been important and interested me during the voyage of my life during which I have always had an active social conscience. I hope that during this invasion our people will have a strong animal will to survive and not kneel to the rising storm. I fear however that these thoughts are foundering like a wreck at sea because the gates are already open and the deluge has started.

The Chinese are smarter more cunning than we are and extremely mercenary. Its one thing to say that education and inter cultural tolerances is the key tools in fighting racism and xenophobia. I agree I have lived with Indians all my life, married one and hate racism (even though I feel different cultures do make life more difficult), but *racism is not and has nothing to do with the problem.*

The problem is that this country of writers and artists is 'up for grabs' by hordes of Chinese trickling into it legally and illegally and taking over this island within twenty years. It would be 'a piece of cake' to do so (while we play the harp and Paisley whistles the old orange flute) and no one knows it better than they.

To explain how this was done in countries now run by Chinese such as the Phillipines is another story. There are many books on the subject and International reports. I am fortunate however in having more stories and plays in my head than I can handle that are much more pleasant to write.

Because the subject is consequential and extremely important if we are to survive I don't think it was intellectual or political arrogance. I am sorry alas for having digressed and perhaps throwing the reader a 'curve', so back to my story.

I married a Colombian girl who proved to be everything a man would wish for. We were a happy pair in the early days. We often visited Myriam's aunt's coffee finca in Colombia, our first stop being Sebastapol where we would spend the night and be greeted by a quintet of guitarists playing Colombian music, through dinner and into the night.

Next day we would drive to the Finca admiring the lovely Spanish style house and the young coffee plants. The branches carried bouquets of small white flowers with a jasmine-like fragrance that was everywhere. The coffee fruit is red when mature and about 18 millimeters long. We wore ponchos as it was cool on the mountains where we spent a lot of time painting. We painted village scenes and village folk whom we loved. Myriam's watercolours were beautiful and I delight in seeing them today. We had many delicious fruits to eat and paint as 'still life'. Home cooked meals sometimes gave us three different meats in the soup (SanCocho) and on the plate.

At home in California we had many friends. Myriam loved to hear me play the bagpipes for dancing competitions in Van Nuys, C.A. On Saint Patrick's Day we went with Pipe Major Sean More Rice (a Hollywood stunt man) to play in John Ford's house whose guests included Maureen O'Hara. There was no end to the weddings and births of Latin friends.

It was a happy loving marriage except for one strange phenomenon, which is that Celtic people who marry mestizas (a female of mixed European and Indian blood) have little chance of having children, if not for that, life would have been great.

Both my 'best man' from Leixlip and my best friend from Germany, who was at my wedding, had Peruvian wives and none of us had children. My best man after two years of fruitless marriage sought the help of his brother, a physician in Leixlip Ireland. The Irish Doctor came up with sad statistics and a sound reason (which I have forgotten) that the odds weighed heavily against the three of us ever having children. He made a joke of it to me saying that I had failed the Irish race!

My wife, unconvinced, spent seventeen hundred dollars having her 'tubes' checked. Her sister in Colombia had twelve kids to feed and was the envy of my wife. I was not at all happy at not having an insurance against loneliness in my old age, besides I liked kids. I went to the Chancery office in San Francisco and applied for an annulment but did not have the heart to pursue it. However thirty years later times had changed and I separated from her.

My wife and I attended Mass regularly as this gave us great comfort. I was never good at mental prayer or praying with beads, so this social act was a sublime 'healing' for me. Afterwards Myriam, who was a very good cook, would make a Colombian or Irish dinner. Housekeeping was like a hobby to her. She and I were happy during those early years.

However I noticed, shortly after we were married, that she had a problem and one day I confronted her about a snide remark she made to her sister for no apparent reason.

"Why did you make such a rude remark to Ruby for no reason at all when we were all having such a nice time?"

"I don't know," she replied.

"You don't know? What do you mean you don't know?"

"I just can't help it, and I worry so much afterwards!" she said with tears.

"Well if you can't help it, you should see a psychiatrist or a priest, because if this gets any worse we are going to end up splitting!"

I said I felt that if one accepts one has a problem he or she is half way to solving it. A thought comes, removes another and as fast as a 'plop' you make with your finger in your gum, it can change one's whole way of thinking suddenly and for ever.

For thirty years I thought something like that would happen. She was not crazy. She had a job as an office manager for under-writers for years. The sight of a fly would throw her in a state of panic. If one appeared as we were having dinner, all the windows had to be opened wide and the fly dispatched promptly. She didn't seem glued together very securely some of the time. Perhaps I was the cause of it as I was not easy to live with either.

If a dog or cat came within petting distance she would stand up and order it to go away or call for help. I had the most good-natured German shepherd which she invariably kept at a distance. He stayed in the garage or outside when she was there. She fed him while I was abroad but seldom if ever took him for a walk. The dog was a big worry while I was sailing.

I converted an attic into a painting studio and have painted for over thirty years and exhibited paintings in the Simic Gallery in Carmel and elsewhere. A few were shown in Dublin such as the Oriel in Nassau Street and the James in Dalkey but with few sales. I never really understood the *business* of art and painted for pleasure. . Eighty percent of paintings are bought by women in California and, strangely, most women do not buy paintings by women. It might be smart (though customs change) for women to use their last name only. Few would buy modern art in the sixties but preferred still life and land or seascapes.

I would sit with the bright Californian sun coming through the skylight and my dog had his favourite spot beside me while guitar music or Beethoven played on the stereo. The dog recognised the purring sound of Myriam's station wagon Fiat car before I could. He could hear grass growing. He would flip down to the garage before she pulled in.

"Has Gabby been here?" she would ask, "I smell him," she'd say smothering a laugh.

"He's too afraid of you to come indoors. You really make our lives miserable!" I'd reply.

She could tell if I had been to the bar by the smell of stale smoke on my clothes.

"You've been to church!" she'd jest. Her sense of smell was remarkable.

When my brother and his wife came for holidays one year there was no place to put their clothes, every closet was full. She still had her first Holy Communion dress and every hat she had ever worn and even the shoes she wore as a teenager in Colombia. Boxes began to creep in to the studio, all numbered and labelled until they blocked out the light. Every shopping bag, bill, receipt, letter, postcard - every single thing she ever received she hoarded. She also accumulated stamps like a collector. She had boxes of stamps she would put into an album when she would retire and have more time. I often wished I could have been able to keep every book I ever read.

One day I got a helper to move her things down to the living room before going to sea. When I returned they were all back in the attic including a huge portrait of my late father, which she had removed from the living room and replaced with a bigger one of her father, a Colombian architect, whose bust was in a public square in Bogotá.

Everything had to be done her way and if not she grew resentful and I thought she might be that way even with God! When she wasn't wearing the victim's cloak, as the saying goes, it seemed she was wearing the martyr's halo! From the day of the annulment of our marriage, until the day her brother died three years later, she went to church but did not receive Holy Communion. She nursed her wrath and ceased to be a practising Catholic as decreed by the Church, and so she did not fulfil what's known as her Easter Duty just to spite the Church or God for granting me an annulment. I think all of our troubles revert back to her being barren. Not being able to bear children, along with my time at sea, though we loved each other, ruined our marriage.

Some sailors wisely marry homely women, so they have fewer worries at sea. I didn't. Soon after my return from duty, I would become restless for Ireland and my family there. I would plead that I needed a short vacation, which was shocking and incredible to our friends. My dog, confused after my absence, would pee on the carpet with excitement. He would bring his plastic container to her for food and give me a pathetic look. We had problems with loneliness, she, myself and the dog, and we ceased to comfort each other and grew cold as the years went by. This was selfish but if there is any defence, I would venture that it is because human nature shrinks from boredom.

I was at a crisis. I felt my church was a sinking ship and my marriage twenty fathoms below. What happened to the joy, happiness and fullness of life that being a Christian meant? When I suggested going back to Ireland to live on my own, I knew I had gone the wrong way about it. 'A sharp knife cuts cleanest.' I should have just gone. Life became stressful.

One day my wife said,

"The car needs gas". Of late she had developed a habit of half filling the tank if it ran out, while I would always fill it. It was a frustration I pushed aside until one day it suddenly boiled up bringing other money situations to the fore that caused arguments. We had had enough.

"If we are going to separate you can go to Mass on your own". I did so reluctantly, like a schoolboy. The Mass was in Vietnamese (which, like Cantonese, seems to fall on the nerves. As Graham Green put it, it sounds like birds chirping). I regretted the Mass not being in Latin, even though some of us may have only understood the Mass phrases, we felt more at home with that language. The sound of the Asian tongue fell on my ears with a feeling of rejection. I simply could not put my mind to it and left before the Mass was over.

Next day I went to the Chancery office. "After all these years, are you sure you want to go ahead with it" said the Chancery Attorney. "Yes" I reaffirmed. It was only a matter of days before I filed for a divorce, and moved into an apartment.

One day, trembling like a leaf from head to foot, I arrived home to find the house empty. Not only was my dog gone, but dozens of paintings which I had done over the years had gone, not a stick of furniture, garden tools, even the light bulbs as if to put the final dot. I didn't know where she had gone. Worse still she had taken the deeds to my home in Dalkey and my private files. My teeth began to chatter like castanets as I tried to figure out whether she had gone mad or not and what would become of me.

My wife had accumulated so much over the years and could not stand losing even a used postage stamp. I felt a long bitter battle would take place as we divided the property. I was wrong because with the help of an attorney I got most of my things back within a week. The divorce was done in a relatively friendly way. There was no fighting or arguing. I am still friends with her and her family though we seldom see each other. I never remarried. After the devorce I left my dog in a shelter for three weeks while I went to Ireland. When I took him out I could not believe the change in his appearance. He was like a skeleton and could not stand properly from arthritis. I had lost my home, my wife and now seeing my dog in such a condition, I thought the best thing to do was to put him down so he could not suffer anymore. I became overwhelmed with remorse and guilt. I was perhaps emotionally unstable and vulnerable, when I met Carmelta Palnka an assertive pretty Chinese women, the most commanding woman I have ever known, a neighbour born in the Philipines.

CHAPTER FOURTEEN

Carmelita

W e were in Saint Mathew's church at high mass. As we sat back after the Credo, a new face, a sallow- complexioned woman of forty five made her way to the pulpit to read the lesson. It was easy to perceive that she was familiar with the house of God, by the way the assistants, sacristan and others made their obeisance to her. They were familiar with the clear and silvery voice that sang the glory to heaven.

She had a waspish Samurai-like trim supple figure, tar black hair with a glowing sheen and eyes sparkling with expression. Her complexion was smooth blending the lily with the cherry blossom. Her cheeks had a yellow blush. She was dressed in a simple beige suit, with a delicate cream blouse. A vague pattern of palm trees and tropical seas outlined in threads of gold on it, which showed her figure to advantage and her toilet arranged so she looked as handsome as she was eloquent. From time to time she covered her left eye with her hand as if to wipe something away.

Indeed her dominion did not consist only of her beauty. The tiny hands counting the beads of her rosary seemed so devout. Her parents and children listened attentively and were proud to have the eldest son, a postulant Cistercian monk celebrate with them. The grandparents, the daughter, and four children paraded proudly down the aisle from the first pew, following the priest and altar boys.

The appreciative looks of the parishioners was one of adulation, in a church badly in need of young members. Her face was strong. Her french was not very intelligible to me when I met her later but her german, which she had learned at school from Austrian nuns in Manila along with English and three Asian languages gained her a high reputation. She worked in the International department of Wells Fargo Bank, San Francisco until she was fired for not furnishing citizen papers. She was an Ivy Leaguer and had met her husband in college.

Two years earlier, before Myriam and I had separated, on a fine morning, with the promise of a beautiful day, I sniffed the freshly cut grass and the flowers. The squirrels scampered out of the way of my fast moving mower and jittered into my kitchen for scraps. It was shortly after eight in the morning. Carmelita was walking past my place. She wore dark brown washed out Bermudas, a faded blouse, well worn tennis shoes and a large straw hat with a black velvet band. Of all the hats women wear, I find none more elegant than a simple straw hat with a nice band. I like it because, to me, it makes a woman stand out somehow in an unpretentious, dignified way. Her muscular legs glistened with a yellowish hue in the bright morning sun.

"Good morning Mr Quinn, I am curious as to why you have a cover on your ear, my husband is a surgeon possible he could help," she said as I turned off the mower.

"Oh, it's a long a story. I worked on a ship. One day I had a probe with a meter taking a voltage reading and forgot that if I put the telephone to my ear I would 'ground' myself and get fifteen hundred volts through my body. It did a lot of damage to my ear, tongue and even scarred my heart. The pain in the ear is 'direct pain' from the wounded tongue. I am attending Stanford hospital and am fed up with doctors. The only cure they could come up with was to stay away from citrus, coffee, tea, booze and cigarettes. Eat fruits and vegetables which at least are cheap, and in time, it would get better. So I was told, but thank you anyway."

As I went to restart the mower, she moved onto the lawn, under the shade of a tree and said, "That's fine, if you are tired of doctors but you know I have an idea I would like to share with you, could we have a coffee later, I want you to meet some of our neighbours?"

"You have an idea? What idea?"

"Meet me in the Bistro at three! Bye."

As I made my way down to the Bistro, the irritation of my spirit in giving in to what I expected to be a 'pitch' or even an embarrassing suggestion (not on my doorstep) gradually subsided and I became cheerfully expectant of a chat. The Bistro was really a bookstore with a coffee bar in the centre, people sat for hours reading over a coffee. It had huge windows so one got the feeling of being outdoors. As I entered the store I paused. Yes, she's very good looking, I thought, as she sat reading a book about wife beating.

"Hello, may I get you a coffee?"

"I'll have an herb tea thanks."

"Did you hear that they are going to close down the Bay Meadows racetrack'? "Do you gamble, Carmelita?" I asked

"Not much, I like to ride and I have my own horse in the Philippines!"

We sat there, the light of the bright blue sky shone above us. After a time she gave me a pitch in the form of an invitation.

"Patrick, if I can show you the best way to make a hundred thousand in a year, you to be the sole judge, would you be interested?" I thought a moment. If I say yes I'm letting myself in for something and if I say no, I must be a fool. I found myself between two stools with one simple question.

Life is all buying and selling. Avoid the pitch and we avoid being bought, I thought. Still I put myself in the way of being sold. Oscar Wilde said 'I can resist everything except temptation'

"Maybe, what's it all about?"

"Next Monday morning I'm having a meeting with David Cohen who will give us a presentation of a new invention, a guitar that teaches one to play by having 'LEDS' small lights where the fingers go. Can you come along, you won't regret it and as I said, *you* will be the sole judge?"

She was silent to let me 'burn' for a minute, and then I said, "I guess I have nothing to lose". As it turned out of course I had a lot to lose.

I found that Carmelita had a remarkable power in the way she controlled others, with her cool exterior, which along with great shrewdness and knowledge of the world, made her a formidable foe. As wc left, she replaced the book on the shelf while I asked her if she liked it.

"I have done work for the University on wife beating. Battering isn't just a matter of broken bones and purple faces and being left with a paroxysm of a battered eardrum. It can wreck lives beyond repair. Anyway it's a lovely afternoon, and would you care to take a walk?"

We headed for Coyote point. She began a tale of herself having been battered in Venezuela to my surprise and having had vicious quarrels with her first husband who was an Engineer. "That explains as to why she keeps putting her hand to her left eye where there was a slight wound," I thought.

"My husband, a Venezuelan, was called a Spanish Jew who, like those expelled from Spain by Ferdinand and Isabella, are to be found scattered throughout South America in Chile, Argentina and of course Europe. Actually the Jewish Settlement in South America preceded that in North America. Marino Jews, who came to the former continent soon after its discovery, especially went to Brazil, in the early settlements. They have mostly disappeared in Venezuela. I don't know why Jews find it difficult to assimilate with other races?"

"That was the excuse de Valera, President of Ireland, gave to the Irish people when he prevented Jews from coming to Ireland during the war, which was a shame. Of course we did not know their destiny," I said.

"Surinam", she continued, "where the Jews were granted tolerance by the Dutch, presented the oldest Jewish community in North or South America. Of course, most of the Jews one meets today came in the latter part of the nineteenth century. A lot of Indian Sephardic arrived about 1850, and only five years later there were anti-Jewish outbreaks in Cora and other towns."

"Really, that's very interesting," I replied.

"My first husband was an Engineer whom I met at Cornell University. At the wedding the guests were exclusively his family circle, none of my family or friends attended the wedding. I took lessons in Judaism. My parents, who are from the Fukiang province of China, are characterised in the Philippines as the 'Jews of China' because of our high profile in the world of commerce. We are the wealthiest group in the Philippines. Anyway I had lessons from a Rabbi. Though I never allowed myself become brainwashed in any religion.

"We had a lovely home in Venezuela meaning 'little Venice'. Sometimes the house shook under peals of thunder, while lightning flashed and a downpour of rain followed. My husband kept my passport locked away, lest I decide to leave the country with the kids after an argument, or perhaps some violence.

I was trapped. One morning, I was preparing to visit the town after I had been to 'Shacharit' (the morning prayers) in the synagogue. My attention was drawn to a conversation below my veranda by two souls sheltering from the torrent of rain.

"I say! Are you the lady whose mother was killed in Poland' a man said?
'Yes why?

"And then they got into a long dialogue of the woes and wounds of the past which I found most depressing. I felt agonised and grieved. Later at the entrance to the synagogue, feeling a little frustrated, I mentioned casually to the Rabbi,

'I am unhappy at the way my Uncles and Aunts keep talking about the Holocaust fully recounting the whole episode as they speak. I hate the idea of my children carrying that legacy. Why I said that I don't know. The Rabbi was a patient man. He gave me a cold stare of offended honour that I can never forget, but he said nothing. I was hurt more by the silence than any words and finally got angry and said 'Rabbi I don't *have* to do anything or even be here if I don't want to'. Then he raised his voice and looked at me in a peculiar way, not straight in the eye, but at the bridge of my nose. I found this quite intimidating. He insinuated that I preferred Latin, the language of the crude Romans to Hebrew the language of Moses! Bizarre! Can you imagine? Then one of the hair clips holding his yarmulke flew off and struck me in the face, missing my eye."

She halted briefly, looked me straight in the eyes, as she took my wrist and said, "Do you know what really bugged me all along about Judaism? I didn't want my children to '*inherit*' all that stuff about the Gas Chambers or have future generations resentful. I didn't wish to inflict *that* on my children's children. This along with losing my inheritances from father upset me."

"You learned a lot about the Jewish religion?" I asked.

"Sure! I can sing the Henei matovu manayim in Hebrew as well as the Regina Coeli or the Stabit Mater in Latin."

"Are you 'religious' or is it just poetry to you?" I asked hoping not to sound sarcastic. "I do have my doubts," she replied.

"What are they to you?" she asked, but didn't wait for an answer and continued. "What's in the head comes out the mouth, so I finally told him the truth that I would be disinherited if I changed my religion to Judaism. He said 'Mula, Mula, Mula, Mula' (money) and walked away. My husband I thought, God! If he tells my husband the way I've been talking he will kill me."

She hastily put her hand over her left eye, as if hoping the heat from it would ease the sudden pain. Dropping her head she tearfully said "Oh God! To think back on the hatred and how my husband was so jealous of me, of his religion, of everything he possessed, He drove me almost insane."

"So what happened, did you have a row with your husband?"

"Yes as time went on things got worse with the Rabbi advising my husband, I actually feared for my life from what my husband might do to me. That evening, at seven o'clock, my dog got the start on us, by tensing and recognising the sound of my husband's car. Staggering, dropping the keys he banged the door of the car. The gravel crunched under his feet as he walked with deliberate and what seemed like interminably slow steps from the gate. Jesus! It was as if my heart pounded painfully in unison with each plodding heavy step as it ground down the stones".

I was leaning closer to her now as we stood, telling her to wait while a Fire Engine followed by police cars blasted by with harsh sounding sirens, lest I miss a word. I put my hand over her eye hoping some healing power would come from the heat in it, while I said silently "God help her, heal this woman, have mercy." All quiet again except for the shrieks of the children playing, she continued;

"When my husband staggered into the house, he slowly removed his coat, hung it on the coat-stand, and as if not to waste time, grabbed a stick and turned it, so the heavy, pointed silver fox-head handgrip could be used as his goad.

The drunken swine attacked me without warning. I used my feet - kicking his crotch, then his ribs, I aimed at the back of his neck then, while trying to ward off the blows, my young son David got in the way. In attempting to protect me he fell heavily. Then my husband jumped on me, dragging me towards the window, which was five floors high and threw me on to it. I banged the side of my head against the pillar resulting in these awful headaches and a life with paroxysms in my left eye. He had every intention of throwing me off the balcony. My boy David screamed in terror.

96

As my husband tried to lift me, I managed to land a heavy blow in the base of his neck, making him dizzy so that his knees weakened.

The screams brought a knock on the door. 'Que passa, abierto el porto' It was like the voice of an angel vigilante. My poor son was the sole, sorry witness and will be tormented for the rest of his life".

"Wife battering doesn't end at a beating, it has many penalties that go on," I said. Her greatest sorrow was that her son witnessed and endured the scene. I liked that and was becoming absorbed in her story and a little bit infatuated.

"What happened then?"

"I picked up a few belongings and went to my-sister- in-law's home bringing David with me. I was in a somewhat traumatic state and I signed over my house to her and she happily promised to sell it for me, for $100,000. She sold the house but kept the money. I never recovered a cent. That was the only way I could get her help and get out of the country and come to the USA. With a two month visa, after I found my passport."

"I left Venezuela for ever and penniless at that. At the airport while waiting for the plane I felt scorned and bitter. I took a pair of scissors and clipped my son's 'Shirley Temple' curls and along with his Yarmulke and Talmud, I tossed them with gusto into the garbage can. I had originally brought $250,000 to Venezuela. My sister- in-law returned my letters. I could not and will never again enter that country"

And thus we walked, as she recalled past experiences. More people were coming to the streets and 'the after work traffic' began to increase. We left the park, reached the road for home. I stopped outside a new Thai restaurant and studied the menu for a moment. It was now almost five in the afternoon.

"It's a good place, do you want to eat?" she asked.

Asian menus are usually so long they tend to frustrate my choice, so I suggested she order while I excused myself to wash the fingers. When I returned there were two large fish on a plate, head, tail and all.

"You already have ordered fish! They come with the heads and tails on?" I stared at the gleaming yellow heads and bluish rings around the scales. "Look at those black, yellow teeth, the fish is old!" I stressed, with a forced smile putting a little pungency on her plate for being ahead of me in ordering while I was away..

"What are you having?" asked the waitress.

"I'm not going to eat something that's looking at me; I'll have prawns, fried shrimp with boiled rice and Swiss Kale". I ordered and turning to Carmelita said.

"How are things in the Philippines, your folks and all that?".

"In the Philippines five per cent of the population own ninety per cent of the wealth. There are five Chinese families, who have so much power, that if they pulled out tomorrow the Philippines would collapse. Marcos has made it a country of house-boys. My family is one of the privileged families living in Macati. "What's that a haven for the rich?"

"Philippinos are immature in tolerating corruption. The government is groping in the dark, trying to find the moral legitimacy to govern in a dirty back yard", she said.

"Really I guess you should know," I wavered. "My father came penniless from China and became a millionaire at nineteen. He fought the Japanese with Marcos, managed to pile and bury the spoils of war, for a later date. "You mean looting?" She ignored the question. "When I was young, he used to read me balance sheets instead of fairy tales to put me to sleep. My father sold a cigarette factory to Lucia Tan, who is worth over a billion now and owns fifty percent of PAL (Philippine airlines). The deal went well for Tan, but I think not for my father. I believe now Philippine cigarettes contain a stronger addictive substance than nicotine. My father refused to do that. Before I was sixteen, I was running several companies in Manila."

She took photos of her stable from her bag. A most impressive one with Mother Therese herself and her father outside a building which she said her father had given Mother Therese as a gift.

"Dinners, fiestas, banquets were the order of the day and the talk of the day in Manila," she glowed. "After each function Father would invite a platoon of servants for the leftovers, until there was a huge gathering on the lawn. He would sit back with a cigar in one hand, a whiskey in the other while the girls served him with passion. I don't mean sex of course, though I'm sure he was ok in that department."

She cleared all the food she had on her plate ignoring the skeletons of the two fish for awhile, then, lifting the tail, throwing her head back and with a bite like a bear trap, bit off the head and began to chew madly, relishing it like a cat with a canary.

"What about the teeth?" I asked. "There is more nourishment in the brain of a fish than in the rest of it; besides it is the nearest thing to a cure for cancer. I have two degrees from Cornell, one in Nutrition, the other in Biology, I also speak five languages."

"O.K. O.K." I answered. I felt a little piqued but why I didn't know. I walked her to her house. In her garden stood her father, an elderly Chinese dressed in a Filipino shirt and Bermuda shorts, his hands were cupped around a huge black rose as he inhaled deep draughts of its fragrance. His stature, broad nose and sensitivity to nature, as he paused, I pictured a painting of a Chinese 'Goethe'.

On the way home we had stopped at a market to get milk and bread. When I reached for my wallet while undressing that night, it was missing.

CHAPTER FIFTEEN

OPTEK

Foster City is not a city but a residential part of the Bay Area, built on reclaimed sandy soil I have never gone there without the feeling of danger that the liquefied sand could be in a quake. Foster truly sowed the seeds for a great disaster by building there. Like my home in San Mateo (where my house was damaged by quake in the seventies) it is on the San Andreas fault. Deep beneath the sand and streets of San Frnancisco for that matter a time bomb is ticking. If there should be a large quake nearby it is now feared that the whole developed area would sink into the sand in one great whirlpool. It was developed by Foster, an Irishman who made a huge fortune on what some considered waist land.

It took fifteen minutes to get to the residence where the meeting was being held to discuss OPTEC (the name of the company bringing out a new type of guitar). The house was that of a fairly wealthy Chinese family. The interior of the house had Chinese furniture throughout, also some Philippine paintings and a large cabinet with Asian glass ware. The bedrooms had gloomy dark furniture with blazing red and blue covers, huge armoires and walk in closets with a host of gay slippers and shoes.

Champagne and appetisers were passed around by the host as a tall youth strummed a new type of guitar which used LEDS (light emitting diodes) and would hopefully become the 'Apple' of the guitar world. There were six guests besides myself, all women. I felt uneasy thinking that I was going to get a 'pitch' and the advantage was on their side since I was alone on their territory. I decided while my glass was filled to the brim that no way would I commit myself today.

David Mendelssohn, the chairman of OPTEK (the manufacturers) and a retired International Vice President for Wells Fargo Bank rolled his sleeves while viewing his Rolex and heavy gold bracelet and gave us the history of the two year old guitar and its prospects of success. He showed a video telling its history and how easy it was to use the computer based instrument, which led the fingers to the keys with LEDS and how it would undoubtedly appeal to the music world market.

It was a beautiful instrument made from African black wild wood, with a complete learning system, so one did not need to read music and it had been on the market for two years. A vice president of Yamaha was 'jumping on the wagon' for sure and joining the sales force or so we were told! As the evening went by I gained confidence that it was truly a remarkable invention. I 'bought the pitch' and ended by climbing on the wagon. I bought shares to the tune of $30,000.00. One backer from the Philippines offered to put a million dollars in. Carmelita, delighted with my investment which put wind in her sails, picked up the phone to consolidate her position and called the President, John Schaffer, who was also C.E.O. of his own world wide aircraft servicing company based in San Jose.

"John, let me have a letter welcoming me on board as director of International Marketing. Show how I fit into the whole thing, giving me something to build our relationship. Don't worry, I will build the business in Asia with no problem at all. But regarding funding, I have a problem. A big funder is offering blocks of money and we can't get him down to about a hundred and fifty thousand. In fact he won't come down to less than two million which we couldn't handle anyway right now. He wants to invest twenty five million. I could have that money this weekend. I have a venture capitalist on hold and another in Canada. We can open a factory in the Philippines which is good."

"One thing, I have to be careful, John, because I think funders have been finding out that I'm starting to move. As I told you, when I came here I had to be anonymous because of the IRS, I can't even have good credit here because they are going to check me out. It's like a dynamite keg, you move it just lightly towards the fire and it will blow in your face. I learned that lesson eight years ago, somebody came in through the back door and blew that powder keg, right into our faces, so I know the feeling and I hate it. Unfortunately people get very greedy. I'm getting a lot of telephone calls although I'm unlisted. Somehow they smell something is going on. It could be lenders who are making these calls." She went on full of enthusiasm hardly letting the President get a word in. No one seemed to be bothered that she was in the country illegally.

"We can raise money by opening a subsidiary in Asia or in Europe. You know if you have fifty one per cent and backing even by my family or Pascal or anybody, I can take care of Asia. That's why we should put it down in writing you know. I can see the potential is tremendous. So we've got to package these things practically and completely under that same umbrella just like a holding company. That is why I'm working along those lines, why I'm giving myself time to retrace the old people, the 'old money' I used to work with. I trust them you see. They keep themselves anonymous and do this very well, because we, after all, were are not only handling big money but we have to know where to *put* it afterwards. We have to know *where to hide it,* we have to know many things and with you I can be frank and throw this at you. You can throw it back at me, you know, so you have no problem". I thought to myself "This may be the way to do things in Manila but here in the U.S.A. things have to be above board and the toll can be high if one plays with the I.R.S".

"Well that's fine, we will do everything to help you" he said.

"That's great", she continued, "I need all the support I can get. I feel like I'm playing tennis with ten players, you know". "Do you have a Fax machine?". he asked.

"No, I don't have a Fax or know how to use one because my secretaries did this for me". At this she gave me a wink as if sitting there listening to her talking on the phone, I was supposed to be glowing.

"Don't you worry the secretary will show you. We will send one over to your home" another wink and a thumbs up.

She called the shots, from the moment she got word that she was to be the Marketing Director for Asia they were all dancing to her tune, like house boys. She did not wait for a letter of confirmation. She called the President's secretary and dictated the format for her contract the way she required it. She inflicted an element of secrecy on people and with her talk of hiding money; she imposed an element of secrecy on herself and on me. I wondered if leaders of industries behave like this or was it entirely an Asian custom.

While getting into her van for home I remarked

"Jaysus you amaze me, Janey Mack! What a performance"

"Why is that and who is Janey Mack?"

"Your control is better than Cleopatra's."

"For sure I have them all in my waistcoat pocket, one day I'm going to own that company."

"Own the company?" I sensed she was the most inscrutable person imaginable. I queried her on her status here in the USA.

"I have three passports, a different photo on each."

"Why three"

"It makes life simpler" she whispered.

I was taken aback quite a lot at such a remark. I believe her parents and their parents and the people from wherever she came must have had a history of great struggle, to become leaders in the world of business and craft. It was, I guessed, not only a family trait, but a provincial one. It was

101

second nature to her to work and control and manipulate people.

Yes indeed, she very well may, eventually and in some devious way, take the whole business from them, if the business were to succeed in a big way; she might do it above board or otherwise I surmised.

The Philippine Mafia, of whom she had spoken a number of times, were known to be in Foster City, where the largest number of wealthy Philippinos live. I recalled that she said 'never threaten me' in a menacing tone and with a glassy look, like a wild animal, suggesting ruthless consequences. She had been talking about her former 'houseboy friends' in Foster City, who had worked as chauffeurs for her father. In fact I had forgotten all about that but as it came to mind just then, I decided I must be careful, I must forget about all this. I may never get anything from it. I don't fit in. I'm more artistic by nature and not much of a business man I thought.

She fumbled with the steering inserting the car key and I realised that I was becoming frightened of this character. I will cancel the cheque in the morning I thought. She knew what was in my mind because she beat me to the bank the next day and lodged the $30.000.00 in OPTEC as soon as the doors were opened. Little did I know that her father's 'old money' was no longer there. Later I heard that he had made some stupid investments, which along with living beyond his means put him out of business. His liabilities were now greater than his assets, which she knew. She herself might not have a pot to piss in, I thought, though I was not convinced. It may have been all show. A week later I received registered certificates for thirty thousand dollars in the mail. Who knows it might end up being the Apple of the guitar world.

* A few years later when the police picked her up she had three passports.

CHAPTER SIXTEEN

Pescadero (a fishing place)

There is one good thing about living in an apartment which is, one can just lock the place up and take off without any worries. Otherwise there are mostly negatives. Early next morning the phone rang. It was Carmelita. I told her I was going to Pescadero to 'view' a house. She suggested having a picnic and using her van so as not to mess up my Citroen car.

"I'm going to eleven o'clock mass in Pescadero."

"May we go?"

"May we go Who's we?" I said

"Myself and the two kids, Victoria and Jane, How do I get to your place?"

"I will meet you at El Camino and Hillsdale at 10 am.or would nine thirty suit you better?."

We climbed route 92 with its spectacular view of the bay area, over the hill between San Mateo and the coast. Here there is a huge reservoir which supplies the bay area with water and reminds one of the Lakes of Killarney for its beauty. We crossed the mountain (known as the hill) and arrived on Route One along the beautiful coast with the welcome sea air and drove south eleven miles on dangerous curves from Half Moon Bay to the two hundred year old Pescadero.

Historical records indicate that many Indians lived there before the Spanish arrived .One could not imagine a more fertile valley with a greater variety of wildlife, and a coast very much alive with crustaceans of all kinds, lobsters, crabs, crayfish, prawns. All the best known molluscs, Abalone was plentiful. Although high seas fish have not yet been 'fished out' one cannot say the same for the shell fish. The rocks have been almost stripped bare from people coming in their thousands, with screwdrivers, picks, and anything that will pry the shell fish away.

San Franciscans love fish of any kind and are famous for crab dishes.

From a once great abundance now we have Rangers watching over the few left that are hard to spot. In the thirties one could have enough abalone shells lying around on one's back yard to cover an entire house, now the shells sell for ten dollars a piece. It is a reminder that the fish source once thought unlimited is quite finite and is in delicate balance. Over-fishing, pollution and alteration of the environment are the chief enemies of fish management. A great number of Chinese keep aquariums for luck and to observe the beauty and behaviour of fish in their homes and seldom is a restaurant seen without a display. Today one may not travel from Half Moon Bay to Pescadero without seeing dead animals and birds on the Highway.

We stopped at a store on the way, which sold newspapers. I asked Carmelita to pick up the 'Chronicle Newspaper' while she got mustard for the ham sandwiches. She said something in Galog to the children while getting out of the van for the store. While she was engaging the owner in conversation, for a somewhat longer time than seemed necessary, I saw the kids busy outside the shop door filling their laps with peaches and taking them to the van. Getting out of the van, I told them to stop or I would tell their mother. They shrugged and didn't seem to mind. They were about five and six years of age, two pretty Chinese young girls with Philippine accents, dressed for the beach. I snatched the bag from the eldest and returned the peaches to the container on the street. No word was spoken in the car or later about the peaches.

Pescadero is an unincorporated village. There is no water supply and the roads are repaired by the village folk. A lot of the people village people are descendants of the original inhabitants, mostly Portuguese, Spanish and some Irish. After we read Mass in the tiny church of Saint Anthony in this one traffic-light, one restaurant (Duartes) village, we headed to the beach which was a mile away and had a picnic in the shade of a big tree on a public table. We had coleslaw, ham sandwiches and corn on the cob loaded with butter and salt, with cokes. I was going to forego viewing the house but Carmelita insisted. I wondered why.

We took a reconnaissance trip around the village. The children passing a house coloured to their liking, or one with a nice garden and a For Sale sign would roar,

"Hey! Patrick there's a lovely pink one with a sign."

"No! Shut up Victoria; look at the yellow one that's nicer."

It was fun. There were many goat farms. We stopped at one where breeds from all over the world were raised. The well known Toggenburgs from the Alps were plentiful. Victoria asked if I liked goats.

"Not especially but I will tell you about a man who did, his name was Paddy McGinty?"

'Paddy McGinty an Irish man of note
Fell in for a fortune and bought himself a Goat
Oh! Said Paddy of milk we'll have our fill
But when he brought it home he found it was a Bill'
"Do you get it?" Naw- yeah- yeah he was a boy goat."

Goats are delicate and have to be carefully prevented from catching human illnesses. The children leaned over a fence and fed the young kids with 'Krispies' while keeping the older goats away.

Carmelita stood watching, looking curiously profound. I'm sure what was uppermost in her mind looking back on it now, was that she was having a vision of being 'mistress of the manor' which of course was her pipedream!

Suddenly she burst out crying, while easing herself down on a rock. When I tried to comfort and lift her, it only made matters worse. In fact she went into some kind of epileptic type convulsion, which must have lasted about ten minutes. I was startled at this reaction coming 'out of the blue'. Little did I know at that time she may have been blaming herself for screwing me because she had burnt her boats from the point of becoming queen of the manor. She may have been carrying a heavy guilt rather than a physical problem.

The quiet pastoral setting had the children and me in a light hearted frame of mind before her outburst. The children began to chide me for whatever I had done to Mamma. They were as puzzled by her behaviour as I was. When she settled down, we had chocolate bars and coke, as if nothing happened, then we all piled into the van and off we went. I had three tearful faces around me and for what reason I knew not. As we were passing a cul de sac my eye caught a house which was only partly visible because of the forest of bushes and trees surrounding it. My interest in the house, which I learned was called the Woodham house, (all houses are called after the original owners or builders) became intense and compulsive.

After permission from the neighbour next door to view it, I carefully threaded my way through the heavy bushes and trees which had the house almost hidden. I looked at the roof. It was damaged by trees growing through it. I would walk away, head for the gate, lift a bush and suddenly spot a most decorative detail! My interest would be aroused all over again.

I became exasperated with Carmelita and the children, because as I turned from the heavy bushes loaded with poison oak and some small snakes with a bright yellow strip a foot long they were right behind me, despite the fact that I had insisted they stay in the van. Carmelita sat at the gate, with her hand over her eye, heeding nothing. I shouted to the children.

"This place is full of poison oak and snakes go back to the van".

The old lime and sand concrete foundation of the eighteen hundreds was turning to powder. That would have to be replaced by raising the house, if it were to be made habitable. I headed again for the gate, then lifting another bush I spotted a lovely old pierced quarter fan ornament on each corner of the porch and on the sides of the supports. Here they were, all back again, behind me. Then the youngest got stung by a wasp, Luckily it was an insect. God! I love children, but I'm not so sure I could tolerate their antics nor have the patience. Then I carelessly grabbed a piece of poison oak and before I could get it away it swiped my arm stung me and left scars for life. Not realizing I had it on my hand when relieving myself it removed most of the pubic hair for good. There is no cure. The Indian cure (I learned later) is to rush to the sea and I understand the sea water can relieve the pain and possibly some of the poison.

I visualised how these rare ornamental pieces would look painted in colours. Now the aesthetics were taking over, while the cost and work of restoration was being shelved. "Glory be to God, restore a house in such a state? Am I gone mad? Let's go," I said.

Then I tried to peek through the window, but the bushes were too dense. In doing so, I noticed the beautiful square bay windows which were common in the 1870s and the delicate tracery on the gable ridge. Colour could bring these to life, I mused. I headed once again to the rear of the house, through the bush pointing out the poison oak, as I made a passage for my retinue. Alas, they got ahead of me and one called out.

"Hi Hi look there's a bathroom".

"What do you mean a bathroom?" I said, "Don't be silly."

To my amazement there was an 'out house' wallpapered with 1800 period paper. A sack of lime still lay there ready for use, and a three seat toilet-one large and two obviously for children, wood for the fire was stacked up ten feet high conveniently beside the out house. Abalone shells completely covered a large work shack, old pieces of machinery and tools everywhere sticking through the high growth.

The following day all I could think of was the aggravation and worry about the children getting hurt and my ivy scars. A week later the house became clearer in my mind. I decided I would buy and restore it to its former beauty, and perhaps open a tearoom for viewers on Sunday afternoons.

With a little research, I found the house had been built by Alfred Winfred Woodhams, in 1870, when he moved to Pescadero. The Thomas Moore house next door was built in 1863. The skeleton of a Wells Fargo Carriage that he drove remained in the yard. The McCormick house, the most sophisticated one, was built in 1869, by James McCormick who arrived here with four brothers and three sisters directly from Ireland. They farmed, bought several businesses, acquired large timber holdings land and became very wealthy.

By restoring the old house, I was not only reviving a thing of beauty, but honouring the memory of our Irish dead who lived and built the beautiful houses on Stage Road Pescadero, a town of four hundred souls. That was an upside bonus and patriotic as well.

I stood to lose money but I had decided and that was that. As I went to thank the man next door for permission to walk around and to seek some information on the owner, I stood aghast at what he had done to his own house. The old windows had been pulled out on the ground floor which meant the front windows as a whole lost their classic symmetry. An ugly two-car garage which was used as a workshop had been added to the side of the house destroying the harmony of the whole building by turning it into a handicraft shop. The house had lasted from 1874 until the fifties before suffering such crass ugliness.

I approached the Historical Foundation for a tax break which they gave me. The neighbour, being a practical journeyman carpenter and having lived next to the house, suggested that demolition was the only sensible thing, he argued so forcibly that I felt he didn't care about preservation and was interested in the land himself. His hardened attitude only helped to support my idea of restoring this building to its former elegance.

Half Moon Bay is about eleven miles north of Pescadero, on Route One which is known all over the world for its scenic beauty. On the way home the hill from the beach became very windy. We were going fast with sharp driving even so instead of lightening the road with chatting, Carmelita wound herself up for another money making discussion. I lay back in the van for a siesta.

CHAPTER SEVENTEEN

Once she had my money
I was a sitting duck

Ihave three plans for making money. I have given a great deal of thought to the idea, but first, I have to put money into the bank in Manila in order to 'move money' from the Hong Kong bank here to San Mateo," Carmelita said."

"What money?" She explained a whole complex system of depositories, negotiable instruments, receipts, the relationship between a fiduciary and principal in large international accounts, how the whole bank works. She telephoned to ascertain the standing of her father's company, the holdings he left to her from his factory and other companies. I understood ninety five per cent, but the important five per cent got lost somewhere. I could not put my finger on it, so it prevented me from asking the right questions.

"If you have a problem with money, talk with your Da. I would like to help you but I just put $30,000 into OPTEX as you very well know. By the way, when I got home from the restaurant my wallet was missing. And there has not been a trace of it yet!"

"Gosh! I'm sorry about that. Let me tell you about my projects" she said while rolling over the subject. "Dick Schneider's father, the inventor of the LED guitar in which you invested, also owns the largest paper works in the USA. Well, Lucia Tan, the man who bought that factory from my father, also bought 49% of PAL and Dick and I are working on a contract to service the airline worth one hundred million dollars. I will get one percent". That's a million dollars I calculated. "If you want to support me I will give you a percentage."

She was now taking the sharp curves of the road dangerously. I felt slightly dizzy and had the beginnings of a headache.

"What do you mean support?"

"I have to go to Chicago to meet Senator Bloomsdale and Paul Jones, the owner of U.S. Paper. I need help with fax and phones, and as I said my money is locked in, until I put something in to move it."

"Would we travel together and then I would meet these people?" "of course!" "You mentioned other projects?"

"Purification of the Pasig River in Manila, I'm working with President Ramos's secretary, the major and prime person on that. We will send engineers from Santa Clara to Manila soon," she said.

"Is that all?"

"No"

"There is a third project?"

"I will explain that later!"

"What percentage would I get?" I asked. "What do you suggest?" she replied. "Sixty forty-you get sixty and I get forty." This figure came to mind because it was what the Galleries gave me for my paintings. I felt great risk, but I thought it worth it since the gains appeared staggering. I was now past seeing risk.

As we drove home, the sun went down behind the hill and dark unsettling clouds appeared on the horizon. Somehow the mountains and the lake were changed to a different form as darkness grew. It was late when we separated after the long day and the morning was already far advanced ere I awoke; the noisy garbage truck was doing its monotonous rounds and making sure everyone had risen. I met Carmelita at the Bistro at eleven o'clock and had her sign an I.O.U. for a personal cheque for $6000. I endorsed it to be paid back in fourteen days, as I had doubts about transfer of funds. Later she had an excuse for a delay in repaying the money that should have put her out of my life for good, but because of my injured aching ear, naivety and foolishness it didn't.

As we left the shop she recognised two Chinese women crossing the street. They hesitated a moment as if to see if they could avoid us. One with a vermilion coloured cap suddenly gripped the arm of the other, who had a black costume trimmed with fur and wearing pearls. She turned her head and appeared to be cautioning her by the stiff image of her appearance and body language. They seemed as if they felt cornered, but decided to come directly toward us.

"Patrick, I want you to meet the daughter of Chiang Kai Shek of Taiwan". I recognised her immediately from her photos in books and newspapers and was impressed.

While they chatted for a while in Chinese, I thought how the Cubans in Miami and the Chinese in Taiwan have one thing in common which is that they both raped their countries before they left, stealing art and valuables. Soon the three said goodbye and moved on. Any qualms I had then about the loan faded and Carmelita regained my confidence.

She drove to a house in Palo Alto and we spent the evening with a man from the Philippines, who could never return there because he had stolen millions from a large company that was owned by the people. They lost their pension funds and yet this family of thieves was living in the U.S.A. in comfort. The house looked like it had a Cecil B. De Mill at the work-over. The owners though friendly kept a distance from me. I might ask too many questions.

We all had been drinking heavily. It had been but a few hours and again I was getting in deeper. From whether to give or not to give, to discussing a percentage, once again *I was on to the route of being had* and was too trusting or stupid to see it.

"Carmelita," I called across the indoor pool, "let's go." Turning around, with one hand over her eye again, she tripped and fell, bruising her ankle on the side of the pool. The host invited us to stay the night, even though we were only an hour's drive from home. She accepted, had more cocktails and enjoyed a swim before retiring. I found a kind of piquancy in Carmelita that was making her mildly attractive, along with her assertive ways in business. If she were successful, according to her, it would bring 'movie money' to both of us and it sometimes appeared she was on the edge of that world by her connections.

However there was one vital ingredient missing and that was a healthy dose of quarrelling and making up? We never quarrelled, she called the shots and I acquiesced. I wanted the business to succeed; I had just been divorced and was craving inner peace. At times I felt I had lost my grip and my sense of reality."I am going to meet Dad tomorrow, the President of Avionics and the Chairman of OPTEX for lunch, you must come"

I drove to Max's restaurant the following day and found Carmelita, her parents and the President of OPTEK waiting inside to be seated. Carmelita spoke to her father.

"Dad, Patrick put thirty thousand in the project."

The Fourth degree Knight of Columbus' ring caught my eye as we shook hands and as I gave the brotherhood acknowledgement. His response was a slightly suppressed horselaugh, as he greeted me. During the meal, Carmelita put the 'screw on me' in such a way I felt obliged to pick up the bill and pay the tariff. By now I had become accustomed to the fact that I was paying for everything, and was being blatantly flayed! *The little they have shall be taken from them*'.I thought to myself.

Carmelita seldom spoke about her husband the surgeon who was in charge of a rehabilitation centre in San Mateo. I later found out that he had to leave suddenly for Venezuela, I understand, because of being unable to account for drugs that went missing. Soon after she moved into her apartment with her two daughters, I agreed to support the business temporarily and was to be reimbursed. The phone cost seven hundred a month. When we visited a Senator or her aunt or Las Vegas I footed all bills as usual. We stayed in the house of the mother of Billy (who was the leader of a group named the Beach Boys). I hurt my back removing a case of wine from the car and was invalided for a couple of days who was a distant relative of Carmelita. He came in one day, we displayed the guitar to him and if memory serves I believe he ordered one. The whole problem was in the merchandising of the guitar. Years later; Yamaha used the same idea successfully.

Months went by, nothing positive resulted in the way of a new business. I got tired of hotels and eating in restaurants. John Schaffer, the owner of American Avionics, who had put a million in OPTEK, in a despairing voice remarked,

"All the travelling and meetings and what did it all come to? nothing". I thought it better to forget about my six thousand, which had worried me a lot, as she was now desperate for money.

One sunny day, after eating in McDonalds with the kids, she suggested moving into my home. In my mindset, from experience with my Colombian wife, I would be slow to marry somebody of another race as I know how difficult different cultured marriages can be. For a poor example, a South American will always back a South American soccer team against a European. This meant that my wife and her relatives would watch the T.V. in the bedroom while I and friends would watch it in the living room, she cheering Brazil and I cheering France. Things like that, which seem trivial, can become divisive in the extreme when occurring on a daily basis. At times I admired Carmelita's talents but I had now grave doubts about her virtues. I did not love her. An interesting phrase in Mary Queen of Scots's book on philosophy states, (while having a dig at her sister Elizabeth), 'talents we admire, but virtue we love'.

"Forget it, we may have had an affair but I will not live with a woman unless I'm married to her, or intend getting married. Besides with two little girls do you think I'm crazy? Men are afraid these days to ride a lift with a kid, much less live with them. Let's carry on as a business relationship", I said almost angrily. She was hurt and I feared her scorn.

*This type of 'third party' scam is one of the most used especially by Kenyans who have made millions by ripping off Europeans. The British and German government warned the elderly not to be fooled by the flood of request for 'bridge money' Requests for a small sum to remove large sums of money is one of the most successful cons.

CHAPTER EIGHTEEN

Rebuilding the house

After spending months of tracing an elderly wealthy lady, owner of the property in Pescadero, who had not seen the place for many, many years, I finally closed the deal. Strangely the rooms were full of furniture from the twenties, some of which were antiques. I found a few old books from the seventeen hundreds and eighteen hundreds. And in fact just about everything one uses for house living, which was a big bonus. I packed all my things into my Recreation Vehicle (it was one of those common Fords that looked like a snail and carried six) and pulled into the front garden of my new home.

For the first six months I had so many problems with the planning department I worked as if I was operating an illicit gin mill! Time was eating up my money and me. I had to keep inspector after inspector at bay while job after job was being done because they told me that I could only spend twenty thousand dollars on the improvements over any two year period. I called for inspections on the worst rainy days. I had 'look outs' and every type of cover-up imaginable in order to get the work passed. The septic tank was so covered with bush, that after they found it, it took the 'Honey Wagon' many hours and more expense to clean it. "This was the second worst job I have inspected", said an inspector from the city. To this day I am curious to know which house was in even worse shape.

I used Mexican workers from the street. They gather in about every town in California, selling their labour. I grew flowers and fruit and many Irish favourites like lavender, irises, zinnias and lots of geraniums, my favourite, with other scarlet flowers. Lilies and daffodils were everywhere. I had apple trees and a very old cherry tree which had little left after the birds had their fill. I had hardy grapes (somewhat sour), magnolias, mimosa, lilac, Californian poppies and other wild flowers.

As work progressed on the house I became more and more reliant on one man named Francisco to supervise the men. He had one problem; he would suddenly take off for a week on five minutes' notice. I became tired and decided to take a two weeks holiday in Ireland. While having lunch in McDonalds before leaving the coast. Carmelita took a two inch supply of napkins, four of which she left on the table, the rest she stuffed into her bag with a supply of 'Sweet and Low' for home use.

"You're doing that in front of the children?" I scolded.

"What?"

"You are stuffing your bag with sugar and napkins".

"Do you wish us to take care of the house, while you're away? The children can enjoy a holiday at the seaside," she cooed not responding to what to her was a foolish question.

"Yeah, Yeah, Yeah," screamed the children in unison, as the first bite of meat stuck in my throat.

"How will they attend school?" I said with mock concern.

"They can take a week's leave. Two weeks later they have holidays anyway."

"Yeah yeah yeah," screamed the children again.

"Where did you get that 'Yeah Yeah'?"

"I'll call you and let you know."

"We can go fishing and crabbing" said the delighted kids. I was not at all happy with the idea but I had to have patience. The kids began talking about borrowing my fishing and crabbing nets and playing with the neighbours next door.

"No, the garage (my office) will be locked up," I said firmly.

"Can we come and see where we are going to sleep?" asked Jane.

I was tired of living alone, cooking and repairing the house at the same time. I had no heating and had to shower in cold water for the time being, until I got the foundation fixed. I asked Carmelita if she would take the children home and come back later for a walk. I wanted to get a few things straightened out not the least the possibility of recovering my six grand.

CHAPTER NINETEEN

A mistake

In Pescadero there are many families who have lived in the same house for generations and not changed or modernised as they do around the bay. Some are born into a home and die in it without anything being changed as if to keep the memory of bygone hopes and to be able to look upon the road travelled.

As we headed in the countryside along under the deep shade of the tall trees sheltered with our sunhats and glasses from the noonday sun towards Butano State park, we came to an old house in a state of disrepair. It appeared uninhabited, even though a wealthy octogenarian farmer, who was born in it, still lived there. We walked past the untidy garden. Carmelita saw Swiss Kale growing among some weeds, as if it were wild. She suddenly took off and went to the rear of the house.

A tall 'forties' looking gentleman in working clothes with expensive crocodile Elvis Presley type pointed shoes, a thick belt with a large Harley Davidson buckle shining in the sun, appeared from nowhere. I stood on the edge of the road somewhat apprehensive that Carmelita might be caught having a pee behind the house.

"What's yer woman doin' behind me house?" he exclaimed.

"I'm damned if I know, is that your house? It's occupied?"

"That house belongs to my uncle, he was born there eighty two years ago. He owns all the land you can see, from the hill over the mountain down to the sea. He is the richest man in Pescadero. His name is Arnez.". He declared snappily.

I thought for a moment he might be hallucinating. "And he still lives in the house he was born in?" I pointed to my house across the fields and said, "I am the new owner of the Woodham house." "I know, your name is Quinn." He snapped again.

God! Where is Carmelita I wondered? Then she appeared from the rear of the house when she heard us talking, she hesitated not knowing whether to hide or come forward. Her hair flying in the breeze, a face with a yellowish blush, from the hard walking in the heavy soil, while carrying an armful of kale, she approached slowly. He looked at her; put his hands on his hips, growing pale, as she slowly walked towards us.

"Good heavens almighty tonight, Lordy Lordy you're taking my Swiss Kale?" He exclaimed loudly.

"Dear me," I said surprised.

She turned to me in a fit and defensively said. "What's wrong with you why do you say 'dear me'? You told me to go and get it, you said it was growing wild" She was fending, sparing nothing or no one to keep face. Then she suddenly roared laughing at my stupefied look, as if she was playing with a puppet. The man grew nervous, his eyes rolled. I shook myself and in an effort to varnish things over and get her out of her imbroglio, I said "I told you the house looked so empty and abandoned, it was a shame to see the Kale going to waste, but didn't mean you should go and steal it."

Relaxing and in a subdued voiced she said "Oh! I thought you meant we could take some". "No No No Nooo", I yelled, blushing deeply, and looking confused. "You misunderstood me. Give it back to Mr. Umph I'm sorry, what is your name again?"

"Arnez, Pete Arnez. My uncle owns the land from here to the sea." Then Carmelita broke into another fit of laughter while Arnez and I looked into each other's eyes at her outburst.

"You mean the whole mountain, cattle and everything? And he lives in *that* house?" I said half jesting and half serious, not being fully convinced. The words spurted out of my mouth as I grew embarrassed at my rudeness.

"He was born in *that* house and the building beside it was his school. It was built in 1851," Arnez said.

"How interesting"

The wealth of these people and the poor quality of life they had, living in a house that still used an 'outhouse' for toilet purposes blew my mind. The land meant everything to them, nothing else meant much besides, I thought. I was his new neighbour. Carmelita spoke as if she was my wife and mistress of the manor. As we started again on the route I said.

"You know, you caused me great embarrassment there just now. For heaven's sake, what are you trying to do to me? Your business ventures have cost me many thousands of dollars apart from owing me six thousand dollars. You are now trying to slander me by suggesting to people we're married while you steal their produce."

It was the first time I had mentioned the loan for weeks and she appeared alarmed as I worked myself into a fury. I had never shown real anger before, and nearly lost my composure. There is always a time when it is impossible to bottle it any longer.

"Are you suggesting I have swindled you?" then turning around she said, "I'm going home."

To my great relief and I hoped it would be a long time before I would see her again. As she walked away, I continued my stroll. I circled the whole village. The wind began to blow, drizzle followed. I could smell it. With two hundred septic tanks in the village it would always be welcome. It was strange I thought how at the same time every day in winter, we would have a chilly wind and rain along the bay. San Francisco weather is much like Dublin. One seldom sees anyone swimming in the sea. The encircling mountains were now being pushed back by a bluish grey haze; shrouding the house. A large gorge many hundred feet deep stood out on one of the mountains with many ridges recently caused by the 1972 earthquake. Occasionally a mountain lion could be seen.

This was a happy place. In the summer crowds would come from all over. There would be fiestas, the Portuguese would have their big church parade, and there would be a couple of bands for the St. Patrick's Day parade. Broncobusters would walk around in their leatherwear sometimes tossing horseshoes; motor cycles would appear in legions. I stopped in Duarte's pub and while ordering a drink I overheard a hurtful remark that my *wife* was caught stealing Swiss kale. I reddened and told myself that it was my own fault for having her around. I must cut my losses and get rid of her otherwise I would never have luck. What a welcome to the neighbourhood! . It was an old west type of 'equalising' town. One did not want to be introduced to it by being caught cropping a neighbour's Swiss kale.

Carmelita prevailed! I agreed she could stay two weeks with the children while I was away.

CHAPTER TWENTY

My money was her plough

"But one thing is, ye know it well enow,
Of Chapman, that their money is their plough"

Chaucer

When I returned from Ireland, Carmelita and the children met me at the airport. A beautiful, friendly Labrador puppy greeted me. Carmelita had paid four hundred dollars for him. They were dressed in new outfits. I asked where this new-found wealth came from. "Father gave it to me." By 'father' she was speaking of a Cistercian Chinese abbot, who had received a farm many years before from her father. He was supposed to be caretaking her property in China.

"Can you repay the six thousand I loaned you" I asked hopefully. "No, not right away but maybe in a couple of months"

Then she showed me the letter (Appendix II) regarding one of the projects. Once again admiring her command of English and her business acumen, I allowed myself to entertain a glimmer of hope. I thought that one of her ventures would come through and I decided to put up with her for a little longer.

"Did you have a good time?" I asked.

"We had great times fishing. We caught lots of crabs and we're going to stay another week until school starts!"

"You can't," I speculated.

"By the way I had problems with the man next door. He was very rude, and insists you take down the fence. He says it's blocking the sun to his kitchen". Francisco planted five rows of beans and one of Swiss Kale and that was all. He stayed away a couple of days. You should get rid of him. By the way a shipmate Captain of yours, Fritz something, called, he said he would come back." I felt the self appointed 'Lady of the Manor' was a Jonah. *She was in fact setting a clever stage, simply to enlist support later on, in case she needed it. She was trying to establish a day to day relationship for what was to come! It was project number three, which she said I would know about later.* I felt the world closing in on me, crawled into bed and slept like a log.

117

The following morning it was unseasonably cold. There was no heating in the house, no running hot water. It was draughty and there was the usual heavy mist from the sea just about every morning. Sunday, I arose early and needing a bit of fellowship went to Mass alone and enjoyed coffee and doughnuts afterwards with the locals.

The subject of the priest's address was 'faith' and how it could move mountains. It was delivered in a husky voice by an old man, telling us to do our duty, and that the lot of the rich was really not much better than that of the poor, because, they too had their trials. I looked around the congregation and noticed a couple of wealthy farmers, and true enough, their countenances said it all! A lot of poor people had been saved from destroying themselves by not over attaching themselves to accumulating wealth. I thought. Carmelita was the living proof of that theory. After Mass the 84 year old landowner Arnez shook my hand and welcomed me to the neighbourhood.

At dusk on Sunday evening, that time of day when shadows are strongest and artists love to paint, the sun was a blazing red as it sank beyond the hills; I told the children to collect their belongings and pack them into the van for home. Then their mother took them outside and she seemed to be coaching them to do something. They went to the porch and began piling everything on my front porch-blankets, toys, clothes, sea shells and other item they had collected from the beach, and elsewhere. Looking at the pile I asked

"What is going on here? Is the van locked?" I went out through the gate, and opened the van door. The kids jumped on the pile and loudly called their Mum. When Carmelita came out, she lay on the pile and began crying.

"Don't hit me! Don't beat me!" Naturally the children screeched hysterically. "Patrick don't you hit Mamma! Don't beat Mamma!"

The commotion was supposed to bring the entire neighbourhood out on the street. However, one could hear 'roars' of a more cheerful kind from every house, and the 'charade' was ignored. 'Come on 'Forty Niners', git him man, git git git im yeah.'. It was the Rose Bowl final that we won. A light appeared on the porch next door. There was silence for a moment. A 'give-away' expectant pause from the crying on the porch, it was clear evidence that they were all play-acting. Suddenly, the commotion started up again.

I stood there confused, I seldom swore as such and an outburst was fruitless anyway. I went to Carmelita, lifted her and pushed her towards the van, she farted loudly. She got in when she realised I was having none of this nonsense.

"Put those things in the van right away," I demanded.

"You don't have to do what that fool tells you!" she screamed.

I felt like giving her a slap across the face. I stood there in silence and in shock as they moved slowly putting things in one by one. Then she roared in a high pitched voice, "Let's go put the things in the van, we're going home". Suddenly the kids were unbelievably agile and moved as quickly as minnows, still crying more loudly now from failure of their plan. I knew at once, there was something seriously wrong. I could see she wasn't out of her mind, because the children were in on the bizarre act. I was convinced she had been 'cooking up' a charge of battery. She was dangerous and would do anything. As the van pulled off, to give impetus not to return, I said aloud, "I'm going to file with 'small claims' for my six thousand tomorrow".

I had been on the brink of a disastrously well-contrived plot but was saved by an act of mercy! A signal from 'above' directed me to banish this witch. Money really is the root of all evil. That's how it started. My luck would change for the better surely, if I rid myself of her. They left for their apartment with the puppy yelping loudly. I was cold and weak from jet lag I had good reason to squeeze into Duarte's bar, to warm up and to cheer on the Forty Niners. America is still a good country. It would be only a matter of time before Carmelita was gone and I would be happy again. When I got home I phoned the Telephone Company to disconnect her phone. That bill cost me thirteen hundred dollars.

Nearly three days elapsed without anything of particular significance occurring. I kept within my wooded retreat and worked leisurely, indeed lazily. I was more amicable with Francisco the gardener and took a Spanish lesson from him each day as the workmen worked on the house. This gave him a respite from the back-breaking job of sowing beans.

It is said that artists have an opinion of themselves equal to the imagination they put into their art, whether they are writers or painters or whatever. Their egos are either enormous, or just the opposite. Artists either love or hate, they seldom feel neutral, their sensitivity to other peoples/feelings makes up for a lot of hurt and their understanding of people makes them natural therapists. It's only art, in my mind, that can put each of us on our own island of peace and contentment.

One Friday Francisco was last to leave after tidying his tools and putting them away with the grace that comes from practice. I poured myself a cup of coffee, more to stop my stomach churning from nerves than anything else, and lay back on my large old wicker chair in the sun. There was quietness about the hills at twilight. I felt as lonely as the Old Woman of Beare, (an old woman who lived in a cave) on a scaffold on a cold day. Here I was building, planting and farming and making a sad business of it and for what?

The following day in the afternoon, while I was removing covers and preparing the septic tank for the 'Honey-Wagon's return, Carmelita suddenly appeared from nowhere with the two children and Max, the dog, in tow.

"Look, I don't want you coming here any more! We're through! If you don't leave I'll call the police and have you removed!"

My neighbour, who was piling wood beside the fences, looked across at me, then at Carmelita. She began to speak rapidly in fluent Spanish to Francisco making it difficult for me to understand. She wanted a confrontation, I realised, for what reason I was not sure. Was I inventing all this? Was there no way now to get rid of this conniving woman?. She was an enigma, I was an enigma, and the whole bloody world was an enigma.

"Look!" I said, "you and I will take a walk, leave the kids here. Francisco will watch them."

I washed my hands which were soiled from lifting the covers of the septic tank and splashed my face to refresh and awaken me with the cold water in the garden. I hoped this second walk would prove more fruitful than the first when she stole the kale and that I would find a way to get this she-wolf out of my life once and for all, no disrespect to the wolves, of course!

As I closed the heavy iron gate my neighbour looked over the fence apparently amused by our countenances and expressions.

'Turning cold,' he said, looking at us from head to toe, taking a dose of self-amusement.

I guess we were a sight. She in her well worn straw hat outsized Bermudas and cheap dirty shoes, which always looked unkempt. She was really dressed for Manila weather yet had a running bluish - yellow nose from the cold. She did not give a fig for convention. I with my rakish cap, tweed coat and blue corduroy breeches?. If his frosty smile meant what I thought, then I suppose we really did make a bizarre couple and a weary scene. No wonder I thought he was vaguely amused and bore a disposition to ridicule as I bid him good day.

We headed towards Stage Street which would bring us into the hilly woods. I cautioned myself to be careful and sagacious. I felt a surge of hope and inexplicable peace at the very thought of getting rid of her. But alas! How? I knew not, she was a millstone.

"I hope you are not entertaining the idea of staying in Pescadero tonight."

"Shall we call a truce?" she said, interrupting me.

"By the way you will be getting your money sooner than you think"

"And that's it," I said abruptly with a hint of impatience.

"Well as I said, you may be getting it soon. Papa is dying and I am going to Manila to fix up his affairs. I hope to send it to you very shortly."

I pushed away her words, to allow the impact to get to me slowly as I feared she was lying and making the usual promises. "When are you going?" I asked.

"As soon as I can arrange to have the children sent to their grandmother in Los Angeles." It was the first I knew she had a mother in LA. We were now going downhill in two senses and were enjoying a comfortable silence. My heart was relieved of a heavy load as the possibility of getting rid of her grew and loomed large! There was hope 'in them thar hills'.

Early the next morning, my curtains always open; I arose, as always with the early morning sun. I prefer it that way rather than being jerked into action by an alarm clock. It was six forty five. The thermometer read minus one degree and there was a heavy covering of frost while the mountains were covered with a pall of fog. Through the window from my bathroom, I saw, away across the field, my wealthy octogenarian neighbour, Mr Arnez, with a heavy parka, hat and scarf, climbing his tractor to start the days ploughing.

My mind digressed to the amount of work I had to do. I looked at the heavy growth around the house and decided to talk to Arnez about the practicality of keeping a goat or goats to clean part of a fenced off garden, since I knew less about goats than Paddy McGinty. I had heard that goats smell, because the males put their heads in the wash of their urine. This is probably done to let the uric acid clean the rubbish hair. In times past people cleaned their hair with urine. Also, I had heard that goats were very vulnerable to pneumonia and I could end up paying veterinary bills, so they might become an expensive item.

In the fields beyond, the remains of pumpkins glistened in the morning sun and lay scattered everywhere. Arnez would plough them under the deep dark rich soil to nourish a new crop which would be sown in April. He ploughed his way to my orchard in twenty minutes and waved good morning from the noisy tractor. He was a special type of human being who had worked as hard as any, for what men everywhere battle to gain. But for a man worth millions, as he was, owning vast properties in Pescadero, it seemed remarkable that such an involvement could continue to be his life.

It has been said that in business 'it is not having the cats that's the fun, but getting the kittens'. I admired the stature of my neighbour, a millionaire out there in the freezing cold living in a house that was still unchanged from when it was built at the turn of the century! 'Nuts' maybe, 'Idiota' no.

My house was six feet off the ground while the foundation was being replaced. I shaved in cold water. Five Samoans and two Mexicans worked over a couple of months. The county did not pass their work because they were supposed to either photograph iron bars in the foundation or show it to the Inspectors before pouring the cement. I came out that same morning to find a large scarlet 'stop work' order pinned to the front door of my house. For some reason, that scarlet warning shining in the glare of the sun focused my mind not on the County Inspector but on Carmelita. A thought flashed through my mind that someone put a curse on me; so many things were going wrong. I was full of angst. I could not help associating the scarlet tag with the woman as if *she* had put it there.

Umph! If only I had stayed with the canvas instead of getting into house restoration! That little tag cost me an additional $9,000.00 to have the foundation reset. When the Samoans realised their mistake they flew the coup.

CHAPTER TWENTY ONE

Umph! That day, that dreadful day!

Instead of a regular bank account, I used Prudential Securities cheques to pay my bills. One day as I perused my statement, I became alarmed that something was askew and for the first time in twenty years, felt Prudential had made some mistake. Examining the cheques, I saw they were made out to 'cash', something I would never do, because if the cheque got lost anyone could cash it. I always made them out to P. Quinn.

Hurriedly, I went through the pile of backlog statements for the previous five months and found cheques to the total figure of $28,400 and all made out to cash. The signature was not mine. I stumbled over a neighbour's dog, who strayed in from nowhere getting to the phone. I called the Security department at Bache. They of course concurred with my finding and immediately closed the account. I jumped into my car, drove an hour's drive to Palo Alto with all my cheques and statements and went to see my 'Security Analyst'. I was assured I should have no problem getting money returned to the account. They gave me a new account and stated that it would be a few days before the account would be credited and my affairs put in order.

That day, that horrible day, began as I tried to figure out who had forged my checks. They were written over a longer period than the contractor was working at my house, so no guilt there. The Mexicans, handier with machetes than with pens, could not have done it as they were 98% illiterate having come from the poorest part of Mexico. I phoned Carmelita, chatted awhile but found no anxiety in her voice. I continued on for some ten minutes, my heart relieving itself as I felt no one could be so relaxed after committing such a crime. Confident that she had not written the cheques, I told her the problem and asked her. "Did you write cheques on my account?" as a closing question, not in the way of a real query.

It did not take long to get her to the point. She was there instantly and without preliminaries in a cold voice. She said with a sudden briskness and acknowledging giggle "Yes I did and by the way, something else, my *father died penniless!*"

As I paused in shock, I felt I had received a smash from a hurl on the head. All was now clear. I remembered finding a second key to my office gone missing. Also, she had an interest in calligraphy (not that it was needed; tellers let signatures go through that seven year old children would notice) and had been a banker. She gained access to the cottage where I did my paper work and I immediately knew she had stolen pages from my chequebook.

"Why did you take the money, you did take it?" I said still hoping she would say it was not true.

"Yes, because I had to" with no panic in her voice.

My recollection of events which followed this dreadful news is vague. For days I was stunned, paralysed, my thoughts went to the chequebook, the stolen key, people about, the sea, the mountains. At Duerte's restaurant, I ate meals I could ill afford. I was sure Bache Corporation, (which I saw then as a victim) would have to make good the loss. They let the cheques go through; they were the cause of my worry. Allowing consideration for my friends there, many of whom I had dealt with for twenty five years, led me to make a fatal mistake; instead of getting an attorney I gave them my trust.

Whether she thought I was stupid or people were stupid I don't know, but Carmelita had the gall to pass by the next day, as if nothing had happened. It was her *third* way to make money, she found my door locked. She moved with an air and ease as if she thought everyone was a thief at heart. It is said that thieves think everyone else is a thief.

CHAPTER TWENTY TWO

A dangerous predicament

I phoned Mr Coyle, the security Chief of Prudential Bache. "I know who took the cheques." I gave them Carmelita's address and phone number. It never occurred to me what the dreadful consequence of my hasty action might be. I know now in hindsight, but it did not occur to me then, that the proper thing to do, of course, was to have phoned an attorney. Not to do so somehow seemed un-American. By contacting Prudential Bache directly, I became the perpetrator and partner in the crime according to them instead of the victim and I became subject to threats and gruelling questions for months on end.

There is a strange statistic in the police departments around the world which is that the higher a man goes in the department, the more years are chopped from his life, due to stress. It is seven years in Hong Kong for a chief Inspector. Policemen on the whole live ten to twenty years less than the average citizen. In the USA a heavy toll is taken on Chief Inspectors when they have a group of detectives working for them and they have to appeal to them to keep working because they are wasting public money, which is in fact equivalent to stealing. There is a nice tendency for Inspectors to show results at any cost even at the expense of a victim so as to slow their lives down. This may explain the pain the security department put me through.

One morning, after a bad night's sleep, (we had all been evacuated to a school on a hill because of an oncoming storm the night before), I was shaving in tepid water while listening to the radio reporting damage done to our village by the rise in the river. Duartes restaurant had two feet of water inside because the riverbanks overflowed. All the houses had septic tanks and the village stank from floating faeces. It was the second time it happened in a hundred years.

The phone rang. Mr. Coyle, the Prudential Bache Inspector, speaking through his nose, an arrogant, over-assertive suburban New Yorker, began to ask impertinent questions. The tone which he assumed, and one that I was unable to reciprocate, gave him an advantage so that I should have chosen not to talk unless he came off his high horse. In a calmer moment I would have hesitated about a lot of things.

"Mr. Quinn, I'm an Investigator, do you know what an Investigator is?" Then there was a pause. I became restless with anxiety as I guessed he was trying to charge me with the crime of collusion.

"Someone is going to go to jail for this, I don't know who," he bellowed. I got angry and roared into the phone.

"What do you mean *you don't know who?* I just told you who forged the cheques. She herself told me so."

Then I received a barrage of questions that left me stunned. How did this woman get your cheque book? Who is this woman? Do you live with her? How did she get into your house? How long have you known her?

"Hang up I'l call you back in fifteen minutes. Don't go away."

Later the phone rang, whispers in the background as to a tape being OK.

"Is your tape OK?" I asked carelessly as a sort of question as to why I was being taped. Then the same questions were repeated ad infinitum.

I reminded myself (while they were deciding whether or not the tape recorder was functioning properly) that I had nothing to worry about. But why did he have the right to be so rude? They were the victim for the money. I became a victim of intimidation. New York detectives think they have the right to be not only discourteous but insolent Instead of co-operation or even being sympathetic they created a frightening scene. I became very worried.

"Have you made out a Police Report?"

"No not yet. My house is five feet off the ground. I'm having a new foundation laid. I'm very busy. You have read in the paper about the storm damage we are having here. The street is flooded and the septic tanks overflowed and the town stinks. Besides, I just come back from Ireland!" I said, hoping to soften the atmosphere since he had a good Irish name.

I found myself on the defensive, why and for what reason I did not know and at a time when clarity and exact precise statements were a necessity. I had jet lag and was not with it. Looking back, I ask, who would be?

"Why do I have to make out a Police report? I told you who wrote the cheques!" I said "She admitted it without in the least trying to hide the fact."

"Mr. Quinn, the linchpin of this whole case depends on a police report."

"A case, what do you mean a case? It's your problem, your money, your pain. You let the cheques go through".

I was about to hang up on him when he lightened his tone.

"She was a Calligrapher you say? Uh Uh. Sounds bad! Who do you think is the victim here, you or us?"

"You are of course; you let the cheques go through. Someone simply walked into your bank and you gave them my money", I said.

Then Coyle the Investigator softened his voice to a slow deliberate suspicious drawl.

"Why did you not notice the drain on your account over what - five or six months?"

On hearing this, I began thinking myself into a sweat. There was a careless aspect to this, which was my not having checked my cheques. That wounded my dignity and I felt like sending Coyle to hell. Instead, in a resigned tone I replied

"O. K. I'm going to call a Sheriff and make out a Police Report, but from here on you talk to my attorney."

I was carelessly and irreverently answering the Investigators ambiguous questions, which I should never have attempted to do in the first place. I could have 'decked him'. I was confused and not evoking the man's sympathy. I had a problem and apparently he had a reason for the grilling. Mr Coyle continued,

"I'm sending you an affidavit. This is a simple form that you will take to a bank manager or a Justice of the Peace and make a sworn statement as to what happened. Complete it, have it witnessed and that will end the matter. You will write your signature ten times, for the Security department to compare the likeness, which will end the matter."

Two days later the affidavit arrived. I lost no time in completing it and returned it by Federal Express. But that did not end the questions and the phoning. I could not work properly and went on as usual until I was sick at heart.

There was no end to the rigmarole. Everyday that went by I assumed my account would be credited. I was teased like a child would tease a puppy with a piece of meat. I continued answering his questions, as my powers of clear judgement diminished by the day. A month went by and my account was not yet credited. I began to fear I might not get any money back. I was too frightened to carry on with the building in case I would run out of funds. I decided to do what I should have done at the outset which was get legal help. I checked the Golden Pages and called an Attorney. I could see that the Investigator, Coyle, was trying to develop inconsistencies, to build a case in order to avoid refunding the account.

I looked at the pile of monthly statements from Prudential, which lay among the building project bills and miscellaneous papers on my desk. I moved the tickets and tags one accumulates after an airline trip, brushed away termite droppings from the old rafter above and while picking up the phone to call the sheriff, I asked myself "How the hell could I have gone five months without checking my statements?"

It wasn't until I opened my mail that I found I had notices from Bache informing me three times, that they had to sell stock to make up the shortfall. I was abroad and didn't open my mail. I looked at my chequebook. It contained multiple entries for cheques for over five thousand dollars to contractors. I put the shortfalls in my account down to this without comparing them with my cheque book. I paid scant attention to the statements, because over the twenty years I had never found Prudential Bache to make a mistake. I felt I was living in a 'Kafka' novel, a man in conflict with fate, spending life among fallen creatures and doing my best not to fall myself. I was in the 'heaviest weather' in every sense.

My house in the sleepy village of Pescadero seemed like a transient's sleeping quarters, a feeling further accentuated by the absence of a woman with all the physical and emotional implications such an absence entails.

The loneliness was like living a half life. I should never have trusted Carmelita. She was the thief who had stolen pages from my chequebook in my garage cum office, while she was a guest and had written the aforementioned cheques and so was guilty of forgery. My thoughts went back to when I first saw her in church. I had such admiration for her Philippine family supporting the cause we all had at heart. Now as I see that while the collection plate was passed around, if she was given the opportunity she would most likely have reverse tithed!

CHAPTER TWENTY THREE

A break in the storm

T ime was moving on and the quality of life was untenable. Meditation on the present and the future grew dark. My old shipmates and friends I heard from rarely. Sailors talk a lot about getting together, but usually see each other only in the Union Hall. The circle of friends and even relatives that I had before going to sea were lost for want of contact and from living on the coast. A strange shyness developed in me to search them out. I had isolated myself and except for a few scrawled lines I was out of touch with people. I looked with consternation at the copies of the twenty cheques Carmelita had forged.

It was a beautiful evening to relax or fish on the beach. I felt suffocated and realised I hadn't eaten all day. I had to get out of the house. I arose, walked across to Duartes (the only eating place in the village and expensive) and ordered oysters with Guinness and a good meal, finishing with a grand Marnier and of course left a tip. I paid thirty-seven bucks all told.

Feeling bloated I came out, jumped into my truck and went 'over the hill' (mountains between the coast and bay area) driving to San Mateo to my old neighbourhood. I spent the rest of the day just chatting. I considered relating the troubles I had. But having a typical practical man's distaste for sentiment, I desisted. It would not be fair to dump my problems on past neighbours, or exploit their affection for me, besides I wanted to forget.

Looking back at my circumstance, if money had not entered into the life between Carmelita and myself and if she had treated me with care and tenderness, I might have been seduced into a tolerable, liveable life with her. Some day she will rue the day she fell out with the law. I just could not bring myself to have any sympathy with her.

An old shipmate, Karl, who had lost his wife was busy cleaning paintbrushes. He washed his hands and we went inside his house. His calm serious look was comforting as he sensed that all was not right with me.

"You're overworking yourself, Patrick, and worst of all, you know you're not going to live in that old house in the woods alone. What's the purpose? Look! Take my advice forget about these fancy ideas, get rid of all the care and worry and go out and spend some of your hard earned money on yourself, disport yourself for a couple of months". Easier said than done I thought.

"Let's go dancing in 'Villa Chertier' or the 'Chez Luis'," he said.

"I just shuffle around, with the same step for every dance, not too good."

"Any man like you who's bounced a wheelbarrow over the turf bogs knows how to dance." I vaguely saw a connection.

We drove down the El Camino. Young people were cruising. There were cars with girls shouting at cars with boys and then making sudden crazy U turns. A school of motorcycles passed led by a police motorcyclist with flashing lights at top speed. The girls perched behind the leather jacket riders with hair coloured red, blue or green as if they were jealous of the colours of the motorcycles and tried to outdo them. The parking lot outside Chez Luis was full, giving promise of a good choice of partners. I was feeling the benefit of the few drinks to get away from the anguish if only for an evening.

The band played Presley period music along with earlier pieces. The older the tunes, the better the seniors would remember them and start singing while dancing. Between conversing, keeping my distance and dancing with a tall blond who danced lightly, I surprised myself by dancing away most of the night.

I will get new 'threads' I thought. A more fashionable suit and will come 'over the hill' more often. I missed San Mateo. The following morning after a cup of coffee and two Farls which I took from the toaster, salted and smothered in butter, I felt I had regained a grip on myself. I had to face thoughts I disliked and people I did not respect and somehow invent a plan to achieve an offensive strategy to get myself solving problems. First thing was to tidy everything around me, put everything in its place. What psychological effect this has, I don't know but it always works for me to focus my mind.

I went to the Post Office to get my mail (old west style) and hastily opened one addressed to me in Carmelita's handwriting. The letter was in a somewhat childish format, asking my forgiveness for what she had done, because she already knew God had forgiven her, but her cunning dawned on me, she did not state as to what she was asking forgiveness for so the letter was useless legally. I picked up the phone and called Carmelita. I taped the following conversation knowing that it was illegal and useless in court, unless the party was informed.

"You stole the money! What did you do with all the money?"

"I spent it on all our living expenses." Her answer was obviously for the benefit of a third party listener because she had not spent one penny.

"You spent it on all your living expenses in six months! You spent thirty five thousand dollars on your living expenses!"

"Our living expenses"

"What do you mean our living expenses; you didn't have any living expenses for me."

"I-I-I mean when we lived together."

"We never lived together. We never lived together, what are you talking about? You lived in Hillsdale, I lived in Pescadero, and when I lived for a couple of months in Hillsdale we had separate apartments."

There is a saying, 'if one has to explain one is losing'. I sensed a 'third party influence' listening. I was being taped so she could fabricate a collusion claim I thought.

"That's what's in your mind! We never lived together! What are you trying to invent? We had a very short lived affair while travelling but never shared the same living space."

Then my mind went blank trying to figure out what she was up to. Was the Inspector in on this or was I going 'nuts'. Could she turn every thing around and get me into trouble with the law and she go Scot free? I had felt an evil undercurrent in the past it was coming into the open. She was trying to establish our having lived together. She was laying the ground for a defence. Was she warning me or trying to convince me not to do anything about getting her into trouble with the police or something ominous could happen to me.

"Can you return the six thousand dollars," I said.

"And you have nothing else to do with me again?" she said coolly.

At this remark I was speechless. How in the wildest of wild dreams could she believe I would want to see her again? It was obviously for someone else's information. A two-minute silence followed. I knew I was being recorded. Either she was a master of self delusion or she was some kind of a maniac. She could not see the difference between thirty five thousand dollars and, say, thirty five dollars? How could she have the nerve to ask such a question?

"So what are you going to do?" I said finally.

"It was in your hands: If you hadn't reported me, I would have given you everything back. Are you actually suing me for the six thousand?"

I didn't respond.

"If there's no chance of seeing you, why can't we at least talk?"

"I'm afraid if I talk to you I'll get into trouble, Bache haven't yet returned the money you stole from my account."

"Well, why haven't they replaced it if it's not your fault?"

"Well that's it. They haven't. I have had no money since then and I have had all kinds of problems here". Then her voice became less business like and softened.

"I will try my best to give you back everything." Now she began to weep,

"I love you sweetheart," she said.

"I'm sorry, I didn't realise." Because she sounded sincere at the moment I gave her the benefit of the doubt. I felt she might have taken the money for our mutual benefit. How easy it was for her to do with her International Wells Fargo experience. I would have gotten my money back and she would have the stolen money. I felt momentarily sorry that her plan went wrong and that she may not have intentionally meant to mislead. Could she have felt this reckless carry - on would bring us together as a family?

I stayed calm, more weeping. Then I said somewhat cruelly,

"You have a problem. You committed a felony and you will get six months at least!"

"Can you tell me you forgive me? Somehow I will get the money back to you". Then her weeping grew and to my puzzlement, she wept uncontrollably for minutes like she did on the outing in Pescadero...

"If GGGod is going to ffforgive me, why can't you? I know God has already forgiven me because he knows I'm going to recompense you." There was sincerity in her voice and I felt I might be missing out on something. Did she break the law for the benefit of both of us by trying to double the money in the bank with stolen money and had no intention of doing me any harm but things went terribly wrong? I. brought forth the thought once more.

"If you had of got an attorney at the beginning that would surely have happened". She said. I didn't respond, knowing she was right; but she, like the attorney, was not aware of Bache's fine print. Suddenly I realised a danger if she skipped town. I felt I had to change the course of her conversation. She was becoming a little incoherent.

Again I weighed the thought, that she could have planned taking the money and the bank would refund my money to me. It would be to both our advantages, *she would have the thirty thousand and I would have got my money back from the bank*. Knowing that I would not go through with such a plan, she did it herself.

"I was so desperate to keep you with me, I did it for you". How stealing my money would keep me with her when she had spent every penny on anything but me, suggested again that she was saying this for the benefit of someone listening.

"You will recompense me," I asked.

"I swear on my father's grave, I will recompense you, can you help me?"

"If I try to help you, I will incriminate myself, I fear the police may be listening in," I said thinking this might intimidate her. I added, "All right, call me again."

"I don't have any money to call you again!"

Could it be possible that she and the children were hungry? It seemed her husband was into drugs, her son was as she had said, was it possible she had a problem also? I asked myself, how could she spend thirty thousand dollars in three months and now be penniless? I concluded she was lying and wanted to have a face to face talk to *incriminate*.

"What did you do with all the money, were you taking drugs?"

"I will pay back the last penny, I swear to God."

"If you can do so it will be your salvation," I said, feeling over-pious.

"I thought we had a permanent relationship. Now I'm in Limbo and everything is worse, now it's a living hell. I need to see you."

Then she wept uncontrollably again. Was she on drugs? I had never thought so before or seen anything to suggest it.

"O.K. Telephone me in a week," I said and hung up.

I had made every effort to be friendly rather than hostile lest she skip and I needed to keep the communication lines open. Mr. Coyle, the Security Chief, came on the phone as soon as I hung up which was odd. Every response I made to the kind of questions he asked seemed to sound self-accusatory. From time to time he asked,

"Did you make a mistake before?" He would mix a statement of their making, with a comment of mine, finding contradictions and irregularities.

They were the Judge and Jury, the best brains of a Conglomerate versus John Doe. What they were going to do was silence me by making a case for collusion and in this way the fine print would become effective and they would turn everything around and make me the victim. If fine print states they are not responsible for losses over thirty days, why in hindsight I ask did their team incur the expense of all this questioning since they lost a mere few thousand dollars? I understood they even sent a Security man to San Mateo to investigate the relationship between Carmelita and myself, according to the Financial Advisor.

I firmly believed the fine print would not have stood up in court. They simply had to build a case of collusion between me and Carmelita, to support that same fine print clause (any funds missing over thirty days would not be paid by the bank) which was crucial to the success of their case. Any forger would be happy to make a case for collusion to avoid arraignment. Carmelita knew more about the business of theft than Bache. She had her plan for defence in her head for years. She was creating events before-hand to support a case for collusion when it would arrive. She worked that plan for a year, and did it well.

It explained many things of the past when she created these events. I became confused. Going to court and dealing with a woman and her two children extremely gifted in the art of creating events, cheating and blatant prevarication, would become a dilemma for me and she knew it, if one faced an economically and racially mixed jury. Besides dealing with a wealthy attorney should Carmelita's brother come to her aid, there would be every chance the prosecution would fail and Carmelita would sue me for slander. But prosecute I would, I decided. At this time I was in a real rage. If the case collapsed she could sue me for slander and so it was not long before apathy set in and I relaxed.

CHAPTER TWENTY FOUR

The attorney

My attorney sat across from me at his huge executive desk. If people in his profession were to identify themselves in their manner of dress, like butchers, bakers or painters, his attire would be ideal. He wore a perfectly fitted, classic herringbone dark grey suit, a silk tie, a gold watch and a ring with one solitary diamond the size of an abalone shell. He was a young man in his forties, confident and professional. At two hundred dollars an hour, he could maintain himself that way.

I assumed that a felony must be pursued on a point of law and wished to be given the facts so I would have a clear mind. In the course of the interview I told him that when I was in Ireland; I had met a Father Shay Cullen an influential man in the Philipines whom I had a conversation about the whole businesss. A very generous man and (he wished to do everything to help me) he is also very influential in the Philippines. He became concerned about interfering without definite evidence that Carmelita had committed a crime or had been prosecuted. To proceed otherwise would put him at risk of a charge of slander. Father Shea said that if we could show that she was guilty he will approach some members of the family to see if he could retrieve some of the money, assuming they are as rich as Carmelita had stated. The family was well known her uncle has a street named after him and owns a big part of a Brewery which is on that very street. The attorney was pleased because he had thought my desire to have her prosecuted was for the most part prompted by hatred and if that were the case there would be no monetary gain and I could get into trouble.

"O. K. that's definitely something in favour of your going ahead with the prosecution" he said. When he asked about my statement not having been checked for months, he remarked "I have never let a month go by without balancing my chequebook".

I admired the shine on his mahogany desk. My file lay in front of me.

The neatness of his office and his sharp eye for detail impressed me. How lucky to be living a regular orderly life, everything as tidy as a new pin, in sharp contrast to my own chaotic existence.

"Have you spoken to the detective about the report?"

"He insisted I couldn't see the report," I said.

"You think there is danger? Listen! I'm a bit old to take any risks, if there is any chance I might get myself into trouble here."

He raised his hand slowly indicating I didn't need to talk right now as he read the police reports.

"Your basic question is 'Should I pursue this prosecution, can I get myself into trouble?' You're secondary question 'Can I call off the prosecution.'"

"Correct," I agreed.

"Let me answer the latter first. The practical answer is 'yes you can'. However, technically you cannot. In the State of California, citizens have the right to pursue a criminal, even if the injured person doesn't want the case pursued. However, although the State has that right, generally speaking, in most crimes there is a key witness without whom the case can never be won. The prosecutor finds it very difficult to prove a case if the key witness doesn't want the case pursued or the key witness is uncooperative. So the result of that is, that from a practical standpoint, if you don't pursue this case it will die. So, if you were to call a detective and say

"I don't want to tangle with that dirty snake, I have decided I don't want to pursue it, I don't want to talk about it, I don't want to supply testimony, I'm too worried, I think she is just going to make my life a hell', then probably that would be the end of it."

"So I don't have to worry about not calling the whole thing off, it will just die of its own accord," I said.

"That's close" he said as he raised his hand again, leaving a slight doubt in my mind.

"Now should you do that? You are wise to be apprehensive, whenever you are accusing another person of committing a crime because if you do that, maliciously that is, because you hate them or you want someone to be hurt by it, you could be sued for 'malicious prosecution' and that occasionally happens.

Now, in order for the person to come after you, for malicious prosecution; obviously if they get convicted of the crime, then they can do that. My concern here is from the things you say in here it seems to me, I would say, that you are less than an ideal witness. It also sounds that she is probably a very accomplished liar. So we can agree on that. The description you have given me previously is that of a con-man or in this case a con-woman."

"That's it, I am prosecuting a con-artist" I said.

"Con - men can turn to their mother and say,

'I'm not your son' and the mother finds herself asking if he really is! You know she will say 'I wonder if he really is?' They're that good at saying untruths and making them sound true." He put his pencil down, crossed his arms.

"So because of all these factors, I must warn you that it could be dangerous for you to press charges. If you honestly think further, that there is a potential that she could beat the case, and not be convicted of forgeries and what not, and then if she turned on you and decided to go after you and accused you of malicious prosecution, presumably the most likely thing she would do is to say that you and she were in collusion of some kind and she was authorised to sign your name so that you could make a claim against Prudential or something like that; the two of you were in on it in other words."

"Yes that's exactly, what she would try to do. That's the scenario that she was trying to create," I agreed. His hand moved to the end of the table. Moments later his secretary entered and asked if we would like coffee.

"Yes please, one sugar, no milk," I said.

"Yes," he continued,

"The picture you paint here. That's what she is trying to create. If you think she has accomplished enough in her lying she might pull that off. I would be very concerned about going after someone like that."

"Well that really is why I am so concerned", I continued.

"She fooled me for so long. She has two degrees and she has experience with Wells Fargo International Department in San Francisco. She told me she taught economics in the University in Venezuela, unless she is lying of course, and I know she has a very good delivery and comes across very positively. Very much indeed" I cautioned.

"That's a nasty combination. I had a little bit of that concern before. The things you described of the incident of her dropping on the ground and getting the kids to pretend you were going to hit their mother, I must say it concerned me as I read it through; I'm not sure how we stand. You know, on the one hand, you don't like to let a crook get away with it, on the other hand, there is nothing in it for you other than cleaning up society."

"Cleaning up society? All I wanted was a bit of Justice and to prevent this happening to others," I said.

"The question is how much are you willing to risk in order to clean up society?"

"I do have a good reason to prosecute," I said, calmly reminding him of Cullen.

"Yes, you don't want to deal with this monster. It sounds like she has exploited you to a great degree. You said she only confessed verbally. We would need something in writing."

"Yes, I have here are a couple of letters!" I handed them to him.

"She says she is sorry for all the harm she has caused but doesn't admit to actually writing the cheques. Has anything else happened in the past that she could say she was referring to?"

"Nothing I can think of."

"You see, I talked to the District Attorney who said if we had a confession we'd have a conviction. It can't be that simple because a confession is a straight shot to a conviction. So there has got to be something wrong with that supposed confession. Don't kid yourself that sitting in the detective's file is a confession that would do you any good. I don't believe there is a confession of any real value sitting in that file. I really don't. Something the detective said may have given you that impression, but if he had a clean confession he would have gone ahead without questioning you."

"Can you get a copy of the report? Don't we have a 'Freedom of Information Act'?" I asked

"I think I may be able to call them and ask them."

"When I called he insisted I couldn't see anything," I said.

"Again, I don't know what good that's going to do you, a report that they are reluctant to prosecute for? Oh yes, from what you told me there is definitely danger. You have to decide whether that danger is great".

"Prudential had their security people here and made a thorough investigation. But the fact that they gave me five thousand of the twenty eight thousand that went missing might be evidence that they knew it was she!" I said.

"Well, it looks like the only thing I might try for you is to try to get the investigator's report. I don't know whether that's available to us or not."

"How would I call the prosecution off should I decide to do so?" I asked.

"Just give Detective Finley a call and say this woman is such a snake, I just don't want to tangle with her. You don't have the power to call it off, but if he hears you've lost interest, he will probably close the file."

"And then, I suppose it can't be re-opened. Shall I call the detective and tell him to call it off?" I asked getting agitated and wanting to get it over with. "Remember one thing, when I told the detective that Prudential gave me five of the twenty seven thousand dollars which went through the bank the first month in forged cheques, he became quite positive and said he would go ahead with the prosecution. Apparently, Detective Finley had assumed I did not get any money, so he suspected they had found some cause for concern.

He probably believed from Bache the Carmelita story, up to that point. But, when he heard that the bank paid me he drew different conclusions."

I tried to be at ease, as I took leave of my Attorney, but was far from it, in fact I was fuming! My frustration had reached a breaking point. I was coming against a brick wall. I had spent a bit of money and come a long way and at great inconvenience and for what? I asked myself. Damn it I'm going to Manila, some one is going to pay. I will talk to Father Cullen, an influential man with clout, who speaks fluent Galog, the man I mentioned to my attorney and he paid little attention to him. I wondered how many poor souls are doing time in this country just because they didn't get justice and took things in to their own hands. God alone knows.

CHAPTER TWENTY FIVE

Manila

8 October 1996

On a hill, in a most fashionable and beautiful picturesque spot in the village of Dalkey County Dublin, the rain was dashing in torrents against the windows. Fitful gusts of wind swept the leaves from the trees and sucked the warm air inside my apartment up the chimney, cooling it. Suddenly there was a bolt of lightning that was so fierce that it ran through the telephone wires, the power lines and, with one direct hit, destroyed all the televisions, computer modems, and video recorders. Even the phones went down in its wake of destruction of all the apartments on the hill of the Sorrento Heights. I missed the California climate.

Frustrated, I thought of packing a portmanteau and heading for sunnier climes, but I decided that the best way to cope was to take the bull by the horns, brave the storm, and walk down to Finnigans for a jar. "A pint o' Guinness is yer only man." Said Miles na Geopleen. Besides I planned heading out to Manila soon and once there I would be only too willing to change the sultry heat the rough pavements and the pollution for the refreshing clime and breezes of beautiful and celebrated Dalkey, with its many castles and smooth pavements. From storms to sultry heat, how little we know of what's going to happen to us any minute of our lives.

I was going to confront Carmelita's family with the fact that the daughter of the Mogul was facing a jail sentence unless they agreed to reimburse me in full. It depended on the situation of her family. If they were middle class, tough luck, if they were 'well heeled' as Carmelita had insisted, I could embarrass them with the thought of a pile of tabloid garbage that would arrive on their doorstep if she were prosecuted. I was on dangerous ground! I must go cap in hand with no suggestion of threats to begin with. The Philippines stinks of feudalism and the corruption and killing at election time is incredible.

When I arrived in Manila, I took one of the colourful, ubiquitous Jitneys which are kings of the road in their mind, and a great example of peoples 'Pop Art'! A statue of the Virgin and another of the Sacred Heart lit up the dash, while a large rosary beads swung from the rear view mirror. A picture of Pope Paul ll blessing Manila was stuck on the ceiling.

I squatted in the four foot high Jitney, lazily observing the dirty crumbling buildings with rusting scarred corrugated sheets and filthy air conditioners jutting out of every room, even onto the pavement. One had to walk on the road to avoid the pumping suffocating heat. Some shacks looked as if they were made from kindling wood, swinging precariously over dirty rivers. One caught glimpses of humanity crawling over garbage in search of food or loot or whatever.

.Except for the Makati inner city, whose skyscrapers one could barely see in the distance through the heavy pollution, it seemed that most of Manila was a large Barrios. There were places here where one could be killed for a bowl of rice as in any other poor city. Yet everyone had a big smile, flashing dents as if to say 'we are happy and healthy, what more do you want?' There were some heart-rending scenes too. People deformed from sickness and deprivation, a lot of which could easily be corrected or alleviated. One could not move without being aware of a hand seeking aid!

Being squeezed into the Jitney for an hour's bumpy ride after sitting long hours in a plane along with the assault on my ears, made me antsy. I felt as if I were crawling out of a trench when I finally emerged, greatly relieved, and headed for the Royal Palm Hotel. In less than ten minutes I was in the privacy of my room. After a welcome shower, I put (as a matter of habit) a hundred dollar bill in my sock (so I would have the means to return to the hotel should I be 'rolled') and locked my credit card and passport in my case which I left in the hotel room. My leg muscles were still bunched. I had a sour tasting coat in my mouth from the rich, salty airline food eaten in a cramped position which was causing reflux.

I walked for an hour to tune the body. I was curious at the appearance and unusual name of a bar called 'Your Other Office' on Mambini Street, I went inside and found well dressed businessmen talking loudly. While ordering a drink I looked at the television and was surprised to see on the screen Father Shea Cullen, forty feet high on a steel pylon which had been erected for transmission lines. He was being interviewed by CNN. He vowed to hold out there, indefinitely, until the line was rerouted. He said that the high-tension cables would pass just above the PREDA, a centre he had opened for victims of child prostitution and abuse and that the lines would emit electromagnetic radiation that could cause various types of cancers to its occupants.

I would never have come without the knowledge that Cullen was going to be behind me while testing Carmelita's family. After seeing Cullen on top of the pylon doing good, (for what I knew not at the time), the moment of happiness was scarce experienced ere I saw the serious look on Cullen's face. Doubts came about my position and whether he would be available for my plans and needs. I had seen a programme on the subject of electric pylons in a village in the States with notice given that people should not to live close to them. This was only one pylon at the school*.

Father Cullen said that Alongapo was run by one family, meaning Mayor Gordon. In Alongapo, the biggest statue in a town, where there are few, is of Gordon's father. It helps to get on in business if one kow-tows to the Gordons. Carmelita had access to Gordon and phoned him quite often. She was interested in putting an International Avionics Service company in the town.

My pursuit was in 'Limbo' if Cullen was not available. There was the problem he might end up in trouble himself for slander, since there had not been a conviction. I was on my own except for his advice and direction which were a great help especially in preparing a precise presentation on paper which I was going to present to Carmelita's brother when putting my case to him.

Soon after I arrived I got in touch with Cullen (who had left the pole after a few days) on the phone before I did anything at PREDA   Fr. Cullen was able to find time to help. He invited me to stay at PREDA so we could discuss my plans thoroughly. I was free to use his office and fax. Unfortunately he said he had no knowledge or acquaintance with the Palanka family. We both got together and put the facts in simple terms, as follows:-

Dear Sonny,

I am sorry to have to tell you that there is a felony charge pending in the United States against your sister Carmelita. This came about because of a number of events which I explain as follows.

1. I came to know Carmelita in the spring of 1994 when she was my neighbour in San Mateo, California. She befriended me and told me a sad story of her life. I was supportive and she told me she was a business woman managing investments on various companies. She ingratiated herself with me and imposed an intimacy that was far beyond the simple friendship of a neighbour. This she used later to make out that I was her intimate and that I colluded in the forgery to defraud my bank.

2. 26th June 1994: Ms Palanka visited me frequently in my house and gained access to my cheque book. Later it was found that she had forged my signature to cheques totalling US$28.400.00. The bank agreed that the cheques were forged and the security camera of the Wells Fargo Bank recorded her cashing checks later identified as being forged on my cheque book.

142

3. October 1994 I filed suit against Prudential Bache and Wells Fargo Bank to recover the sum as they were responsible for allowing the cheques to be cashed without comparing signatures. In October 1995 Prudential Bache and Wells Fargo Bank took limited responsibility and repaid only $5000.00, legal fees cost me $3000.00.This payment by the bank is evidence that a felony took place but they were able to limit their exposure because of a small-print clause. They did not file charges themselves.

4. November 1994. The police investigated and took a statement with charges that would lead to prosecution which is the last thing that I would wish to happen and I am hoping that you could find a way to help me recover my lost retirement funds. This has left me in dire financial straits because due to this I lost my house. Ms Palanka also misled me in believing in the viability of a company making computerized musical instruments when in fact it was more of a con game and I lost $30.000.00 on that which has put me in even greater financial difficulties.

5. Ms Palanka admitted in a letter to me that she had wronged me and that she asked my forgiveness.

.6. The complaint against Ms Palanka is pending in the office of the police investigating officer in San Mateo. I am distressed because of this and would like to appeal to your most honourable and respected family to help me recover the full amount stolen from me, through the forged cheques, by your sister.

Patrick Quinn

I had a bill with Manila telephone numbers phoned by Carmelita when she had my support and phoned most of the numbers. Cautiously, I asked if I had the correct number to identify the name. This way I got quite a few of the people she had phoned and the following day called them again. After the third call I made a warm connection. "Oh, this is Mrs Concertina?"

"I'm a friend of Carmelita, your friend in San Mateo and I have mislaid her brother's phone number, could you help me?"

"Why don't you phone her?"

"I tried but she is not there."

"Just a moment", she returned and after a few pleasantries gave me Carmelita's brother's phone number and his address to boot. It was prudent not to phone him from PRADA. After all there may be more than one criminal in the family and they could trace me if things went wrong.

I took a Jitney out of the area and walked to what would be the makings of a Mall some day. It was dark and it took a few seconds for my eyes to become adjusted and my legs to adjust to the uneven, unsightly pavements which are full of holes. Between a beverage vending machine and a four foot high pink pig, that squeaked and swayed around and went 'honk honk' as two children fought to climb it and even that was guarded by a security officer, a man sat beside a phone that rested on a table. He made his money by charging double for a call on this, his 'private phone', which had an extended lead to the pavement and rested on a box. I awaited my turn.

"Hello, may I speak to Mr Palanka please?"

"Mr Palanka will not be back for two hours, who is calling?"

I was not sure whether to believe her or not. I was dealing with Chinese who were fearsome of kidnapping and hard to contact. Philipino Chinese are the most kidnapped people in the world. It was recently reported that more than half the crimes are committed by the police in Manila.

"My name is Patrick Quinn; I'm a friend of his sister, Carmelita. Tell him I will call later."

My heart was beating wildly. I forced myself to remain calm. A beautiful, very petite girl with scarlet cherry drop lips gave me a sly wink as she brushed her breasts against me while I paid the few cents for the phone. She smiled at me and seemed amused to see me melt. "Why the hell don't I drop the whole thing," I thought, "take an hour's trip over to Angeles City where the Americans live? Am I reliving the past over again, shortening my life?" I took a walk past a bicycle repair shop, tiny bakeries, and carpentries all trying to make a day pay a dollar. I returned after an hour to the same phone.

"Mr Palanka, my name is Patrick Quinn, I'm a friend of your sister, Carmelita and would like to meet you for a brief chat, what time would suit you?"

"What about, Mr. Quinn?"

"Well it's an idea I want to share with you! Would tomorrow suit you or would Wednesday be better?"

"Well, let me see, make it eleven tomorrow at McDonalds of Green Hills. We can find someplace to eat nearby."

"Fine, that's great, I will see you at eleven thirty outside McDonalds tomorrow."

I hung up the phone quickly and nervously while realising that being in such a hurry, I did not discuss how we were going to identify each other. I intended to place the aforementioned statement with the facts on paper in a concise way on the table after we had ordered the meal, putting the onus on him.

I left my Irish passport in the hotel and carried my American. It would be a scandal for the family if it became public that the Mogul's daughter was going to be prosecuted for theft. I knew it was a long shot. I did not want to look back in time and realise that I did not do everything possible to get the funds returned.

On May the 13th I rose early, crossed Makati City in a Jitney and arrived at McDonalds of Green Hills at ten thirty. I perused the area in case of the need for a fast getaway. While doing so, I noticed two guys with an 'instamatic' camera sitting on a bench. I dismissed the thought that they might photograph me perhaps for a later time. I think I was getting frightened.

As a seaman I was used to 'shifting scenery' and working in all kinds of settings but I was beginning to see 'shadows'. As I walked around in the thirty four degrees heat I began to sweat, just as if I had a bad case of the flu. My voice box had changed from the choking effects of smog. Fumes from the Jitney and traffic gave me heartburn. I did not want to leave the area to look for antacid tablets in case I would get lost or be late. I rolled my tongue around my mouth, to make the saliva excrete and then like a child I swished it around between my teeth, as if using a mouthwash, until my mouth was full of saliva. I swallowed slowly and gradually the indigestion symptom disappeared. I was dehydrated and didn't have a hat on my scalp which was burning.

Everything around looked threatening, I suddenly thought what if Carmelita's brother spoke to her in the meantime and would arrive with 'bully boys'? At the thought of this my knees weakened. I stood there for another fifteen minutes. A small dapper man, wearing a dark suit and striped blue shirt appeared. He had a great part of his cheeks concealed behind an immense pair of green spectacles. No mistaking the resemblance because of the light-hearted way he shook hands, I knew he had not been in touch with his sister, to my great relief.

He chose a Chinese restaurant. I had no appetite and just wanted to get this meeting over with. He ordered jumbo prawns, wine, boiled rice and flan for dessert. "That's just fine for me also, except make it a Pepsi without ice."

"Now Patrick", he said, "what can I do for you?"

"Well, I don't have good news and in order to make things more clear I made these explanatory notes," I said as I handed him the summary. As he read my eye fell on a large ring with his initials surrounded by small diamonds. I was not sure if they were real. His gold watch had the tiniest worn area that suggested gold plating. He was very neat but when I saw his shoes, I concluded there was no real money here. I regretted not sizing him up first as I could have refrained from giving him bad news because he looked like a decent man. I silently swore at Carmelita and her materialistic family. I told her brother that I had known his sister for some time as a neighbour and friend, and met his parents. How she and I met for coffee and lunch and how impressed I became with her business acumen, that I invested, with her recommendation, thirty thousand dollars in the OPTEC company. I finally told him about the traumatic experience I had when she confessed to stealing twenty eight thousand dollars from my Prudential Bache account and how the bank refused to accept responsibility for letting forged cheques go through there bank in San Mateo. "This is very sad indeed. He said .We have all been wondering what happened to my sister for months. Her mother is very worried. We don't know where she is. You know if I weren't a religious man I don't think I could have lived this long. My father died, a brother shot himself accidentally while cleaning his guns, another was shot by a lunatic and another died in a plane crash. If I had money it would be an easy solution but I can't do anything about it. I'm sorry Patrick." "That's too bad, I will leave it with you", I said and in no way implying a threat. Two days went by and I had no response. With the least of expectations I mailed the following letter.

Dear Mr Palanka,

I thank you for meeting with me last Tuesday and for the frank and open discussion regarding the problem caused by your misguided sister. I am also a person of principle and religious belief like you and determined to find justice for myself and my family name in such a way as to cause as little embarrassment as possible to anyone else.

I respect you and your family who are well known and highly regarded all over California as an honourable family and that is why I flew around the world from Ireland to visit you personally and reach a settlement

The forgery of cheques to the amount of $28.000.00 and the additional unpaid amount of $6000.00 which was borrowed from me under false pretences constitute serious crimes in the United States and I am looking for a peaceful and just settlement, in order to solve this without undue publicity and hardship for both our families.

I will be content if you and your family can help me recover my retirement fund by making a small monthly payment on behalf of you sister Carmelita I feel that the sum of $500.00 a month until it is paid would be fair and just. I will appreciate if you call me at the following numbers.

Patrick Quinn

At least I was satisfied knowing I had done everything I could to retrieve the stolen money. The following day I took a taxi from a part of the city marred by sheer unrelieved ugliness, to the residential, heavily secured, luxurious oasis of Makati. My first experience as we crossed a ramp to enter the vast residential area came as a shock when security guards demanded and held my driver's licence. I directed the driver to Carmelitas's father's residence and in this area of luxury homes arrived to find a vacant lot where a house had recently been demolished.

The Palankas had gone bust. There were two gardeners working in the house next door. "Is that the house of Mr Palanka? I asked "Palankas, yes they've all gone, this house belongs to the Uncles. They are part of the la Todena Company!" said the gardener. Every one in Manila knew the Palankas, which is why I found it surprising that Fr Cullen did not. La Tondena was a brewery in Ceasar Palanka Street and I understand Carlos and his daughter were part owners. It was this daughter's house I had seen in ruins. Carlos was now living in Las Vegas.His daughter's full name was Sylvia Palanka Quifino, a director in the family brewery business. Because of the fear of kidnapping, I could not get to see anyone. I decided to write and give what I understood was an aunt of hers an account of the meeting with her brother, as she might wish to have her relative saved from incarceration. I mailed the following letter

Latondania Co'

Carlos Palanka Street.

Dear Sylvia Palanka,

I phoned your office on the May 16th-your secretary informed me you were not available. I left a number for you to call. The matter for your consideration is important, indeed urgent, should you wish to save your relative Carmelita from incarceration for felony. On her own admission, verbal of course, she forged my signature on cheques stolen from my cheque book. Her brother has been briefed on all details as the enclosed explanatory notes confirm.

He assures me he is sympathetic, but is not in a position to help financially, yet fully understands the gravity of the situation.

Your part in this unhappy affair is quite straightforward and clear cut. My stolen retirement money must be repaid, I insist I be reimbursed in full. Should you wish to confirm the entire authenticity of this affair, my friend Father Shea Cullen at Preda Foundation Inc. Alongapo 2225573 will gladly supply any further details you may require. He will leave you in no doubt about the reality of my painful experience at the hands of a Palanka

Sincerely

Patrick Quinn

An article by Catherine Cleary on This involvement which was in the Irish Times is in the Appendices (Appendix III).

CHAPTER TWENTY SIX

Once a thief one is always 'on the run'.

My financial advisors, Prudential Bache and keepers of my retirement monies for twenty years allowed forged cheques pass through their system and did not notice or stop even one of the false signatures. I always made my cheques out to P. Quinn, not to 'cash'.

"Don't worry, you will get your money back: they are only playing games." Not only was my attorney no match for the Prudential Bache legal team, but the statute had almost expired when he discovered, in pesky fine print, a little known clause which states, *'customers must check their statement monthly, the bank is only responsible over a thirty day period.'*

In other words if cheques are forged beyond a thirty day period (mine was over two months before I checked it, having been abroad) then 'tough titty', too bad for you, the bank will refund the first thirty days only of those forged cheques. So if a cheque goes through five minutes after the thirty day deadline, one could face a lifetime of poverty and instability. Thirty days after the cheque is *written*, not after it is run through, is the deadline.

Tellers allow false signatures to pass through which a child of ten would notice, thieves walk up to the counter and are handed cash, yet the bank claims it is not responsible! So, if going abroad, or if sick, or dying or before drawing up your will, do they, the bank, go Scot free should a forger enter your securities account? Yes, they do.

It happened to me when my hard earned retirement money went missing. It appeared common knowledge among my friends that the bank would be responsible irrespective of any time lapse, but this turned out to be false. Approaching the statute date my attorney informed me that he would have to settle for a mere $15,000 then $10,000 and finally I was paid $5,000.00. Whether this is a an 'all in' figure or not and by that I mean, could the Attorney also have received a cheque from Prudential Bache for services rendered, I don't know but he charged me $3,000 for collecting $5,000.

I feel that I have not only been ripped off by the bank, but have grounds for legal action against an incompetent attorney whom I unfortunately picked from the Golden Pages. Clearly the interests of justice are not being served when old folks who have worked hard all their lives and have paid their taxes conscientiously are treated shamefully by white collar crooks behind executive desks are little better than rogues. Why can't huge corporations like Prudential Bache Securities be responsible for their lapses in security, and not have us, their customers, pay for their mistakes. Few people and not even my attorney knew of the fine print they hide behind

In my case the forged signature was almost a carbon copy of the real thing, but there are cases where cheques with blatantly false signatures were accepted and passed as normal. Not an eyebrow was raised! Cheques with false signatures that even a ten year old child could spot!

Having been a client for twenty plus years and using Prudential with the 'American Association of Retired People' I am completely disillusioned. Yet there were more surprises to come. I experienced great hardship in doing my civic duty as a prime witness because the city was hesitant to prosecute for some reason. My effort to protect other old folks was slighted and for what end or why, I don't know. Such a woman as Carmelita could over the years relieve many more victims of thousands of dollars without even turning a hair.

I have given a circumspect and just account of how I lived through the traumatic experience of finding myself face to face with a thief in my own back yard, who not only forged cheques on my account, but who knew more ways to mislead a man than the devil himself. It is interwoven with my life story because an adequate understanding of the trauma is impossible without knowing something of the character as well.

The financial loss, the home grief, the difficulties and vicissitudes of trying to gain satisfaction by establishing the identity of the forger and then discovering that even if she were prosecuted, which I thought would be a simple matter would turn out to be such a difficult task that at times I even feared that I could end up in jail myself for someone else's crime, someone who had tried to strip me of my money and reputation and even to blackmail me.

Banks cannot handle embarrassment. For example, they will have one 'put away' for a five hundred dollar heist but send you flowers if you take a million to keep you quiet. It seems that if you relieve a bank of a million dollars, you will be treated like royalty. They will do nothing because the last thing they would wish is that customers suspect their money is not in a safe and secure keeping.

The toll is high and the bridge long if one is to get justice and satisfaction for the crimes of others and the suffering thieves can cause. It should be a salutary lesson to others, lest they too suffer the same disappointment, chagrin and resentment, which may prove even worse than the financial loss itself.

Two primary reasons incited me to write. Firstly to record the strangest enigma in my life, my father, about whom I tried to solve some of the mystery surrounding a missing period of eleven years in his life we all loved and knew the true character of the man. I should be amiss if I had failed to leave these words and recollections to future generations.

The other reason! What happened one day, a dreadful summer's day, 13th May 1995. A felon, a Philippine, stole part of my retirement fund! Little realising when I first saw her in Saint Mathew's church, San Mateo, California the drama she, an 'Ivy leaguer', was to bring into my life, and how she became a fugitive for many years.

AIB has taken customers' money illegally and the Prudential in the U S A. was in court over taking not millions but billions of dollars so what about your money in the regular bank account, is it safe? I ask the reader. *Is your money safe in the Bank*? Be advised, the answer is a resounding no, not at all.

Not only is it not safe. But if you try to recover your money, there will be a sort of veil drawn over your life, as you try to cope with criminality which leaves one bewildered and alone. Their security department will attack as if you yourself were the guilty one, as if somehow you had stolen the bank's money, when the reverse was true because they did not live up to their promises of making good cheques that had been forged. I was even accused of writing the cheques myself (collusion) and threatened many times with a prison sentence on the phone by a detective in New York.

Let me give realism to the attendant circumstances in which I find myself today. After writing off thousands of dollars to an incompetent attorney, I feel there would be more likelyhood of Neapolitan Police finding a pickpocket than retrieving stolen funds from a bank. Justice escaped me. My attorney had said for two years: "*Do not worry you will get your money back: they are only playing games.*"

Not only was my attorney no match for the Prudential Bache legal team, but the statute had almost expired when he discovered the little known clause which states, '*customers must check their statement monthly, the bank is only responsible over a thirty day period*'.

This script is to account for the years where there was a sort of veil drawn over my life as I struggled with criminality, bewildered and alone. Carmelita was jailed for another offence ten years later and my object here is not revenge because I believe '*once a thief, one is always running*'. I believe I have been avenged by the remorse she must suffering.

When I got a subpoena to go to court after ten years my attorney said "All you're doing now is cleaning up society!" That was what attorneys were for (I guess he doesn't vote either) I thought. I felt that at this stage of my life, I would take his advice. Why go through all those troublesome 'tapes' of the past in my head again, just 'to clean up society' My 'Irishness' would have me clean up society even though it might be dangerous., and I lived alone.

The human eye always falls on a sharp line, be it on a painting or a horizon. Some writer remarked that the most romantic words in the English language are 'over the seas and far away'. Whenever I felt sad or confused, I would go to the beach focasing on the entwining colours of the sea and sky and the allure of the waters themselves would divert my attention away from my problems to happier memories as a marinar. What better way to travel than by ship? I was quite happy, until a big bank, Prudential Bache/Morgan Stanely, kept a chunk of my retirement fund, and in so doing made life miserable for me for many years. The end of the affair was on 29 January 2002 after receiving a subpoena to be in court to prosecute Palanka, I forwarded a letter to the municipal court in San Mateo. I forwarded a letter refusing to atten the court. (Appendix IV).

EPILOGUE

I was asked;
"Why did you write this periodical memoir?"

I replied that there were times when I was truly submerged in rage and did not know which way to turn. I knew in my heart I would not leave things as they were. If I did I would find it difficult to live with myself. At six in the morning sitting at my computer, another day passes, another day older. I feel, having been asked about this work, emotional as it is, that it has significance and outlines an experience of practical use, to the reader.I believe it does. As I began writing, I was positively aching with pain, a troubled soul.

Because of my distress the urgency and vitality of its importance grew in my mind. I wanted everyone to be aware of the jungle I had come through, and post a warning sign. The theme was already there. There was no need for the 'inward flash'. The characters were there too, no need to invent. All I had to do, was jog the memory, get the 'boilers' going and the nightmare, now past, came to life, and vividly at that, all the way to my childhood. In retrospect I think sometimes, if father might have embraced me once in his life, this work would not have been.. But that's all too simplistic unrealistic and just a thought. As I finish this book, I regret the more pleasurable time I would have had rewriting my novel. One cannot forecast how much time a memoir is going to take or how harrowing it can be. It is usually written in the sunset years and speeds them away. A friend said "You know I did my B.A. and my thesis was just a couple of scribbles compared to your work". This was a welcome and comforting statement. I believe most self-educated people like me at times feel that those with the Degrees must be smarter. I was an easy target. I became too trusting.

I have long since given up the sea, except to have it in the eye from Sorrento Heights in Dalkey, in the lovely coastal environs of County

Dublin. After forty years in California, I get carried away when coastal storms hit Dalkey and remind me of the S.S. American Trader. This ship was exceptional. Most officers and masters I found to be very alert, willing taking great pride in their ship and the welfare of the crew. America was good to me. I'll finish with God bless America, honour to Ireland.

THE END

Appendix I

Father's obituary

Although he had a sound reputation as an educationalist, he was one of the chattiest men in Dublin, and knew every 'character' in the city. In his later years one of his side-lines was reading for an organisation that examines books for submission to the literary censorship.

The I. R. B. was an Organisation which was a sort of liaison between the Fenians and the 'old' I.R.A. So there may have been a lot of friction in the family because of the very dangerous life he had chosen, while serving the country. This doubt has continued to the fourth generation now, towards the end of the last century, during a kind of interregnum between the original Fenian organisation and the reanimated body, led by Thomas J. Clarke and his colleagues, who were so largely responsible for the insurrection of Easter week, 1916.

The I. R. B. was organised in the provinces, and Pat Quinn is described as secretary to the province of Ulster. Among his colleagues in Belfast I.R.B. circles were Robert Johnson, a veteran Fenian, who died only two or three years ago and father of the poetess, Anne Johnson ('Ethne Carbury' first wife of Mr.Seamus McManus), his son, James Johnson, Henry Dobbyn, and the father of Mr. Dennis McCullough, now a well known Dublin business man.

Among many bodies to which P.J. Quinn acted as secretary was the Belfast Celtic Literary Society, of which 'Joe' Devlin, once famous as M.P., was a member. But I do not think that after the turn of the century he had much part in revolutionary activities.

Certainly nobody looked less the revolutionary than Quinn did. And there was little of the schoolmaster about him.

Appendix II

TO: Mr John Schaffer,
President American Avionics.
Dear John,

        I have reviewed and evaluated your proposal to PAL and feel that the most crucial point of the proposal has to be re-emphasized.

        Lucy Tan, being hard headed business man will obviously want to protect and enhance his big investment in PAL. One of his biggest priorities will be the relations with both Airbus and Boeing to delay delivery of the
aircraft on order. Since you mentioned to me on several occasions, that you are a personal friend of Harry Jandorn, Chairman of Airbus Industries, PAL through you, would be very effective in helping PAL negotiate with Airbus Industries.
Likewise with Boeing you would provide PAl with the support and help them
with the 747's.

        As I see it, both Boeing and Airbus would feel more comfortable
knowing that RAS will be taking an active role in turning PAL around,
making negotiations much easier with both manufacturers.

        I believe that now is a perfect opportunity for Lucia and PAL to turn our airline into a respected international carrier.

        I will be expecting the proposal package by DHL by Friday sent to my address:- 444 South El Camino Real #44, San Mateo CA.94404 as we agreed. I will be enclosing in that package a hand-written letter for Lucia and by the end of next week will have the package delivered by hand to her personally by a member of my family.

        I look forward to a mutually beneficial association in the years
to come. Through our sincere efforts and hard work, we can achieve it.

                         yours truly,
                         Carmelita Palanka.

QUINN-RAGE

Appendix III

Article in The Irish Times

Father Shea Cullen, the Irish priest campaigning against child prostitution in the Philippines, will complain to a human right commission about his treatment by a local police. He says he was beaten up, handcuffed and held for six hours without medical attention last Wednesday night.

Last April he built a perch halfway up the 90-metre steel pylon. His protest and the successful prosecution of paedophile tourists have attracted widespread publicity.

During the incident, Father Cullen said, he was manhandled off the perch and handcuffed with his hands behind his back. He was thrown into a van by the policemen, who were out of uniform, and taken to the station where he was held for six hours. He was not seriously injured. 'They robbed us of our radios, cameras and a cellular phone. One of my senior staff had a gun cocked to his head, with live ammunition'. Fr. Cullen said there was a large number of witnesses and they were preparing statements. Yesterday, the Fianna Fail TD for Dublin South East, Mr Eoin Ryan called on the Tanaiste, Mr Spring to, intervene on Cullen's behalf. His campaign for justice has disturbed a powerful and corrupt circle in the Philippines. International opinion is a powerful force in securing his continued safety. Father Cullen said he received no medical treatment in custody. 'No doctor in the city would give us a legal medical'. The city was controlled by one powerful family.

They are infuriated with our success in prosecuting paedophiles. We have just found and arrested an American Paedophile who is wanted for six charges of incest and child abuse in the United States'. Father Cullen said he had been successful in halting the electricity project for three months. He said he felt the routing of the electricity line directly outside the orphanage of thirty children was 'almost vindictive' There were 16,000 prostitutes in the city, he said, and countless numbers of children involved in the tourist trade 'We have 211 cases now pending'.

Fr Cullen said the protest would continue and he would lodge a complaint with a human rights commission in Manila. Asked whether he was concerned for his safety he said, 'I certainly was last night because I thought they were going to stage an accident. I was 40 feet up the pole, with my hands tied behind my back; they could have dropped me and said I was trying to escape.'

End of article

Appendix IV

808

Laurel Ave #105

San

Mateo 94401.

29th

January 2002

The municipal court
San Mateo
Dear Sir,
I wish to appeal to be granted the option of not attending the court because of the following reasons.-
It is now over eight years since I filed against the plaintiff.
I am now a seventy year old bachelor living alone in a one-bedroom apartment Co-Op being treated for HBP.
The mental anguish and suffering of the past would be painful to recall if I have to go to court at this late stage.
After filing against the plaintiff, I went to the Philippines and, with the aid of the Reverend Father Shay Cullen we located her brother. He said that he had not heard from her for a long time. I got the impression that she came from a good family.
"Once a thief one is always running" I believe by now she has been avenged and punished by remorse. At this stage the right thing to do is drop it.

Yours faithfully
Patrick Quinn

Once a thief, one is always on the 'run'
Something is wrong with the whole system. I had the greatest difficulty having patience when I thought of our Jury system that might judge more by appearances than logic. At least that's what I understood, when he said I might not look like an ideal witness, but I guess he meant the way I presented myself on the whole
In Europe I understand they have a three Judge system which is as

sacred as the American ideology. The fact was that with my case, when I left the attorney I felt I dare not appear as a witness for the state because I would not know what to expect. I had doubt and uncertainty.

How can people with non-legal minds like me be expected to make a sound judgement in a case like mine, which is the American system? A system with three Judges would, I feel, deal more expertly and fairly with my case, because they would be experienced. I would have more confidence in prosecutions simply because they would have been trained in their metier. They would have studied law for years before practising or making judgements. Of course, they might be open to bribery (there only being three of them) but there is an Appeal Court and if there were three more judges then there would be six altogether as in the case of a trial by Jury.

The point is, isn't it better to have three men, who know there metier than six persons who are only learning? I would prefer three such men who know people than a hundred apprentices. I was on a jury and found difficulty understanding what the Judge was telling us. Watch this, not to do that, think this way not the other, not to discuss this or say that. It is quite obvious that having 'street people' deciding on what's necessary for a good and sound judgement is risky. The Judge was trying to teach in a short and emotional time people who are nervous, as any one would be starting a new job, the tricks of the trade and not the trade itself.

Three men with experience in such matters who know their metier and not just the tricks of the trade would in my case be a better choice. However, I don't know the legalities nor do I have a legal mind but as a victim I am frustrated that Carmelita was to go free and Prudential Bache for that matter. The Jury system over the centuries is a clear statement of democratic values which modern tyrants too have sought to deny. But my experience of an attorney makes me fearful of pursuing justice I am more than a little disgusted.

Conclusion

An autobiography is like a will, one's last testament. This is a semi-autobiography. Though I probably had enough ego to write a full autobiography, I was too unsure of myself to make this a long work to try the reader's patience. I didn't intend to bare my soul, but 'brush in hand' for the first time as a writer I hoped to use bold strokes.. In the past year I have tried to mingle fact and fiction while writing a mystery novel, but it is still unfinished. So what! It's the involvement of writing, painting and music, my way of sanctification, praying, that helps ease the tedium of what Premier Francois Mitterend described as one of the saddest things he knew, *an old man living alone,*. In this work I do relate to the following:-

The life of everyman is a diary in which he means to write one story, and writes another; and his humblest hour is when he compares the volume as it is with that he vowed to make it. J.M. Barrie